Quilling for Beginners

*A Step-By-Step Guide to Learn Everything You
Need to Know On the Contemporary Techniques,
Patterns and Tools of Paper Quilling
In a Quick and Easy Way*

By Brenda Sanders

Disclaimer

All erudition supplied in this book is specified for educational and academic purposes only. The author is not in any way in charge of any outcomes that emerge from using this book. Constructive efforts have been made to render information that is both precise and effective; however, the author is not to be held answerable for the accuracy or use/misuse of this information.

Foreword

I would like to thank you for taking the first step of trusting me and deciding to purchase/read this life-transforming book. Thanks for investing your time and resources on this product.

I can assure you of precise outcomes if you will diligently follow the specific blueprint I lay in the information handbook you are currently checking out. It has transformed lives, and I firmly believe it will equally change your life, too.

All the information I provided in this Do-It-Yourself piece is easy to absorb and practice.

Table of Contents

Introduction

Paper quilling is known as paper filigree. It can be defined as the art of rolling paper, especially when quilling it, folding it into diverse shapes and designs, pasting it on paper, and making a stunning three-dimensional piece of fine art. It is finished using slim portions of shaded papers, folded into a quilling needle, framing an ideal shape, and finally, the shapes are glued together to form objects.

It is an art highly known for its aesthetic purpose and is commonly used in making jewelry, fancy boxes, greeting cards, flowers for decorating walls, and much more. Lately, it has become a popular part of art gallery exhibitions.

The interesting thing is that you don't need to break your pocket to take up this hobby successfully. You need some basic supplies, but others can be improvised until you can afford them all. You could equally make do with some paper around you, cutting them into strips of paper for your project; this is if you can't access already cut paper strips.

The art includes loads of complex designs that could easily get you frustrated if you don't have the right materials or have knowledge of the basic shapes and how to make them. This book will guide you on the basic shape you need to begin with, and the complex shape you need to master. The starting point is the making of coils (closed and open) from where other shapes and designs surface. Once you've successfully learned this, your journey as a paper quiller begins, and with consistency, while trying out new projects, you'll find yourself at a professional level soon enough.

The origin of paper quilling as an art can be traced as far back as the 16th and 17th centuries. It is believed to have been practiced mainly by Italian and French nuns, whose love for decorating religious objects spurred them to find even better ways of doing so whilst saving the little money they had.

They made use of gold-gilded remnants of paper trimmed off in the process of making books, and this resulted in fine-gold quilled works at the time of emergence. This was a beautiful alternative to golden filigree, which was very expensive at that time, and so was not readily available.

The practice found footing in England in the 18th century with the development of paper, which was then accompanied by the use of vellum and parchment. The art soon became the favorite pastime of ladies who were often referred to as the "the ladies of amusement," a term used to point out ladies who had no house duties and equally had no inclination to take up jobs.

They would often make use of their created designs/quilled works to cover screens, tea-caddies, frames, etc. it soon became part of the curriculum in female boarding schools. It was not practiced then by working-class ladies as they saw it as an art of leisure. Eventually, it also sailed its ship into the United States of America, where it temporarily lost its voice to other more ancient hobbies, like knitting, sewing, painting, etc. The craft further gained footings across the Atlantic with the help of colonial masters who moved from countries to countries, their women bringing with them their favorite pastime routine of quilling.

Despite the odds faced centuries before, the art is now a well-celebrated part of the world's creativity, and this is thanks to the ability to learn anything easily via social media and books. The popularity can also be attributed to its usefulness in children and adult craft, making it possible to keep kids creatively busy in schools and at home. And also, providing awesome pieces for decorating the kids' room, making gift-giving special in a different way, thus showing your loved ones how special and unique they are. Starting is pretty easy; as long as you are interested, you're ready to invest the time needed to learn and the basic materials.

There are a variety of ways to give life to your paper quilling ideas; the use of exceptional 3-dimensional designs is currently the way some unique paper crafters prefer to do their job, others prefer simple tilts towards the less-complex designs, preferring to make earrings, pendants, and others. For others, it is better viewed on canvas in art galleries, and yet others prefer the magnificence of museum walls for the exhibition of the work.

Regarding tools, a variety of simple and complex ones are available for purchase in the paper markets. Some, you can do without; others, you can improvise for. Either way, you won't have any issue sourcing for required materials as a beginner. It is equally advisable as a beginner to make do with the basic tools needed to learn, and then, as time goes on, you can further purchase more complex tools.

Paper quilling is a work of art that is finished by cutting paper into long strips and folding and cutting the pieces into various shapes and attaching them together to frame enhancing artistic ideas. When the paper is moved around a plume to make a basic curl shape, and then, attached at the tip, it's basically known as paper quilling; these molded loops are organized to shape improving blossoms, cards and diverse fancy samples like ironwork.

The Importance of Paper Quilling

Paper quilling is exceptionally straightforward brightening craftsmanship that even a fledgling can ace in an hour or two. In spite of the fact that only your creative mind can limit the potential outcomes, the beautiful pieces can be basic or complex relying upon your assurance. Yet, one thing is without a doubt, paper quilling is the ideal art project anybody can begin anytime. Regardless of whether you are only an amateur, you can accomplish the best outcome in the blink of an eye. Moreover, the discipline cost is practically close to nothing, so if, you are hoping to begin it as a relaxation action or a wellspring of salary, paper quilling is one of the most significant artwork you can wander into without the slightest hesitation about putting resources into it, in light of the fact that the ornamental artistry structures can pay ordinarily more than you put in.

Chapter 1: Types of Paper Recommended for Quilling

On the off chance that you are an amateur in this art, it's likely that you may, at one point or another, settle on an off-base decision with regards to the correct sort of paper material to use for a particular sort of work. Be that as it may, it's likewise applicable even to the individuals who appear to be experts in this art.

A few people will in general buy papers in open markets, online shopping centers, or grocery stores, and do the strip cutting without anyone else with either scissors or the convenient paper shredder; and there are other people who simply feel free to get the already-made ones.

This is a fundamental thought to set up before picking a specific paper. This means it has to do with the accessible thickness of the paper as it goes far to influence the external appearance of your completed task/work. For better comprehension of what this implies, here is a breakdown of what the content weight paper strip and the composing weight paper strip are about. Demanding that this will help the assurance of the beginner who thus would be glad to see his/her undertaking come out great without a lot of pressure.

Paper is fundamental in quilling everything, reflected in the title. You could purchase both pre-cut paper strips or genuinely cut the pieces yourself. There are advantages and terrible drawbacks to the two styles of paper strips, with pre-cut paper which is essential and productive anyway, being fairly more exorbitant than DIY paper strips.

Pre-Cut Paper Strips for Quilling

You can purchase quilled paper in a pre-cut structure, saving you time and power from measuring and cutting. Quilling units for juveniles customarily join pre-cut strips.

Making Your Own Paper Strips for Quilling

Through cutting paper strips yourself, you will save money with the pace of time. What is fine is that you may use additional paper you may have from various sources. You will moreover have the opportunity to apply paper that changes in tendency, surface, or models.

The Way to Make Your Personal Paper Strips

There are different strategies to make your own paper strips: mechanical or manual. The mechanical strategy uses a shredder, while the manual system fuses cutting paper with a decreasing device involving a couple of scissors, a sharp edge, or a paper trimmer.

Regardless, when you decide to move the manual course and use scissors, a ruler and pencil will be required to help measure. In case you use a paper trimmer, you will have the choice to stay away from those extra resources.

A shredder can have the alternative to make strips for you quickly, but will no longer have the ideal edges which you will require for your masterpiece. This methodology may also not be prepared for getting you the right width you liked either. Purchasing a shredder for paper quilling can in like manner be difficult. I wouldn't use a shredder to convey strips for paper quilling. It is by and by not a dependable system for creating splendid, solid strips to apply to your quilling pieces.

What Sort of Paper Do I Exploit for Quilling?

Pre-cut strips will ordinarily be available in paper with an appropriate weight. In case you are cutting your own strips, I would urge beginning with paper weighing 120 grams (grams per square meter) as it is valuable for rolling and making shapes. Regardless, you could use something from 80-160 grams for paper quilling.

Other master quillers would suggest that, as a tenderfoot, you can use the precut-paper strip for your first undertaking.

Advantages and Disadvantages in Using the Precut-Paper Strip

At the point when you start your paper quilling works, you will soon notice that getting or requesting precut-paper strips (already-made papers) has a lot of negatives when contrasted with its positives.

A few people might oppose to this, but you realize everybody has his/her preferences as this is mine. Along these lines, you reserve the privilege to oppose, but as a matter of fact, making your paper strip is much better as it opens you to an enormous chance/space to finding out more and more grounds in this specialty.

Preferences:

1. It is efficient. This means the time you would have used in cutting/making your own paper strips will be spared and preserved for other positive use on the task or something else.

2. While utilizing the precut paper-strips, it is exceptionally simple to deal with and situate for potential safekeeping when essential.

3. The issues of deciding for a paper brand and shading when you are locally sourcing for your quilling materials.

4. It can likewise make your work neater. This is as indicated by some quilling specialists, they think that because of the way that some of these precut are all around bundled and flawlessly cut, they go further to make your work slick and progressive.

Disservices:

Like the saying goes that everything that has advantages, should most likely have disadvantages. So it goes for the paper quilling precut paper strips.

1. Initially, when you start, it happens that you have available all you truly need to begin this trip (especially the precut), but you may feel that the already-made papers are anything but difficult to get a hold of, as you would prefer. Be that as it may, that isn't the situation!

2. When you happen to be in a condition where you can't lay your hands on your favored precut paper shading, surface. and brand, you end up getting abandoned and disappointed with the task. Also, if care isn't taken, you may end up pulling out from this exquisite specialty work, even before you begin.

3. Another thing that may intrigue you and simultaneously be a source of stress to you is that you don't have the foggiest idea how to cut your paper yourself.

Chapter 2: Basic Shapes and Rolling Paper

Start with Basic Shapes

Start with basic shapes, similar to the roundabout paper curl. Expand upon this fundamental structure as you ace the ability to make a spread of shapes like the paisley, tear, marquis, tulip, or slug. You can crush, squeeze, and manage the moving paper loop's degree until you get the quilled shape of your preference.

Here are some helpful rules for developing the key moved paper loop:

- Add some of the paper into the space of your device, and with your thumb and index finger on both sides of the paper strip, keep it up with even strain as you switch device in reverse or advances.

- At the point when you reach the end of your paper strip, take it off the gadget. Ensure you don't wind it too firmly; else, you could find it a bit dangerous to take it off the device.

- On the off chance that you simply should make a free curl shape, you may allow the paper loop to reach out before getting rid of it from the gadget, yet if you need a tighter loop, don't allow it to harden before you take it off.

Move Beyond the Shapes

Whenever you have made the energizing shapes, cross here and play around with them. You may:

- Use them to embellish a welcome card.

- Make alluring, carefully assembled studs.
- Create outlined fine art to include a scramble of shading and imagination to your dividers.
- Create 3-dimensional figures and miniatures.
- The openings are perpetual!

Building up a bloom is one of the most straightforward quilling activities that will let you get the elements' grip. Simply watch this method:

- Make two flimsy portions of shaded quilling paper to make the focal point of the bloom. Cut a much more extensive strip—double the slenderer strips' width—for the bloom petals.
- Using a quilling needle or toothpick, make a nice move off the slenderer strip. Then paste the end part of the slenderer curled strip.
- Incorporate another slender strip and move it around the main roll. Paste the end of some portion of the strip to make a firmly moving center for the blossom.
- Now, make cuts all close by the more extensive strip half of the strip down its extent. Add the paste to one finish of this strip and move it over the firmly moved blossom center we made in the first step.
- Paste the finish of the greater strip. When the paste is evaporated pleasantly, use your thumb and palms to overlay the petals outward. That's it—your blossom is done!

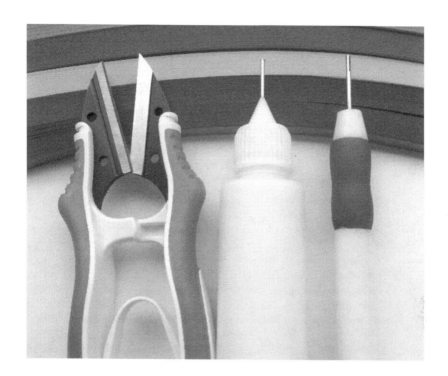

What You Need

- A slotted quilling tools
- Quilling glue in a needle-tip bottle
- Scissors
- Tweezers
- Package of quilling paper strips—for beginners, I recommend ¼-inch wide (it's easy to grip and manipulate); once you've mastered the basic shapes, you may prefer narrower strips. Cut the strips 8½-inches long for this tutorial.

Open and Closed Coils

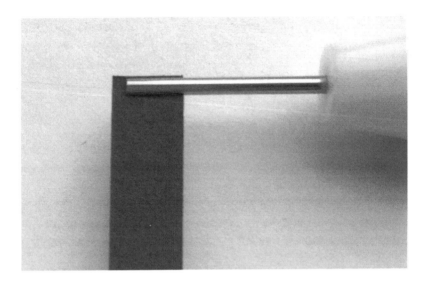

Simple circles are the basis for most other shapes you'll create.

1. Insert paper into the tool

Insert a piece of quilling paper into the slot of your quilling tool; try to line up the paper's edge with the edge of the slot as perfectly as you can. A slotted tool will naturally leave a small crimp in the center of your coil. If you'd like the crimp to be more visible, allow the paper to hang slightly over the edge.

2. Start rolling

Roll the tool with your dominant hand towards your body or away from it (whichever feels most comfortable) while holding the strip taut with your other hand.

3. Glue it

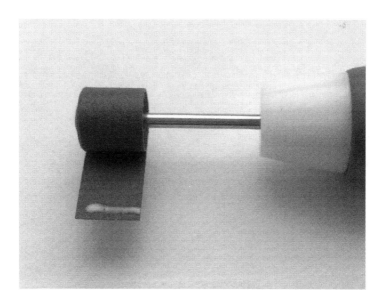

For a closed coil: When you're almost done coiling, place a dab of glue near the end of the strip and roll to complete. You don't want it to expand after you remove it from the tool.

For an open coil: Finish the coil, remove it from the tool, and expand. Once it has fully expanded, add a dab of glue and press the strip down carefully to secure it.

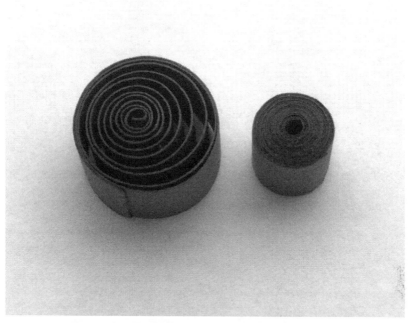

Teardrop

Make an open coil, then place it between the thumb and forefinger of your non-dominant hand. Arrange the inside coils evenly or however you'd like.

With your dominant hand, pinch the paper where you want the point of the teardrop shape.

Teardrop Variations

Basic shapes can be manipulated to create even more shapes. The teardrop is an excellent example of this.

By slightly curving the teardrop around your thumb as you shape it, you can create a subtle shift in form without compromising the center coils. To exaggerate this effect, you can wrap the teardrop around your quilling tool or another cylindrical object.

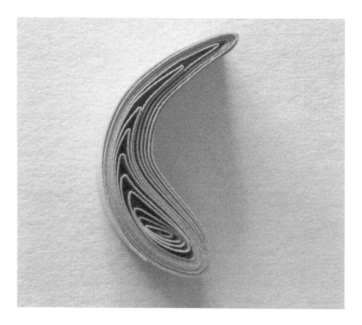

For a more obvious curved shape throughout, press the shape around your quilling tool. From here, you can easily create a paisley shape.

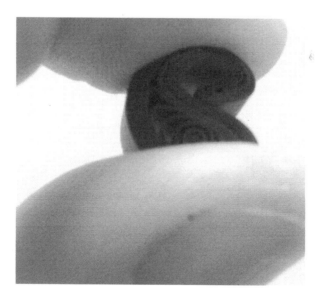

You can curl the shape from the point to the base by rolling it between your fingers.

So many shapes!

Marquis

First, make a teardrop shape, then pinch the opposite end as well.

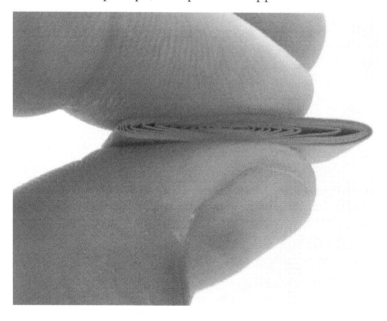

The final shape will be determined by how much you pinch or press the coil together and where you place its center.

Play around with different placements and pressure to create lots of marquis versions.

Tulip

First, make a marquis shape, then turn the shape on its side and pinch a center peak with your fingers.

Slug

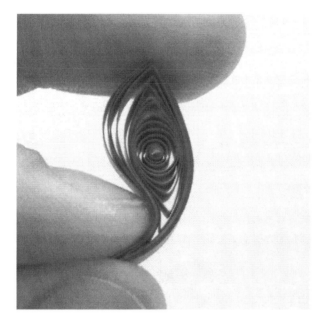

Start with a marquis, then wrap one end around the tip of your finger or a quilling tool.

Do the same to the other end but in the opposite direction. It looks pretty for a slug, doesn't it!

Square or Diamond

Create a marquis shape, then rotate it 90 degrees and pinch both sides again. This will create a diamond shape.

If you want to continue to make a square, gently open up the shape between your fingers.

Square Variations

By playing around with how much of each corner you choose to pinch when creating your square, you can get very different results.

Above left: By applying pressure to the outside corners, you can create a square with a rounded center.

Above center: This was made by completely pressing the open coil together on one side, then opening it up and pinching just the corners on the opposite side.

Above right: This got its unique center by completely pressing down the coil on both turns.

Yet another variation on the square: You can make these by applying pressure to the outside structure with your fingers or the stem of your quilling tool.

Rectangle

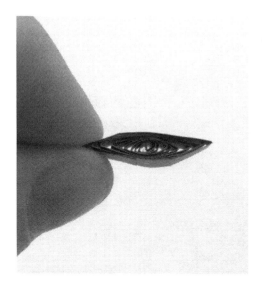

If you can make a square, you can make a rectangle. The difference is in how much you rotate the marquis shape before pinching additional angles.

Rotate it only slightly (rather than 90 degrees) before pinching and then open the shape to reveal the perfect rectangle.

Rectangle Variations

Otherwise, you can create a quadrilateral shape by making your four corners at uneven intervals.

This shape is especially useful when you're making quilled paper mosaics, and you need to fill in an odd space.

Semi-Circle

Start with an open coil, then pinch two corners while leaving the paper above them round. You can also do this by pressing an open coil onto a hard surface like a table and carefully sliding your fingers down the sides. Try both methods to see which suits you best.

Curving the shape's straight edge will allow you to turn a semi-circle into more of a crescent moon shape.

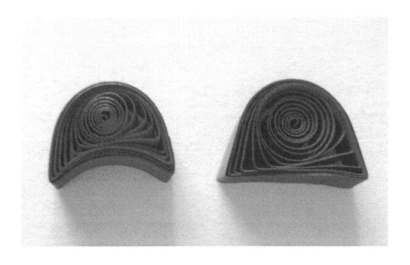

Triangle

Make a teardrop shape, then pinch two additional angles using either your fingers or the tabletop method.

Once again, try both to see what works best for you.

Triangle Variation

To create a shape that resembles a shark fin, press in two sides of your triangle and leave the third side flat.

Arrow

Make a teardrop, then pull the center down towards the base and hold it in place with your fingers.

Using the long side of the slotted needle, press down deeply into the base.

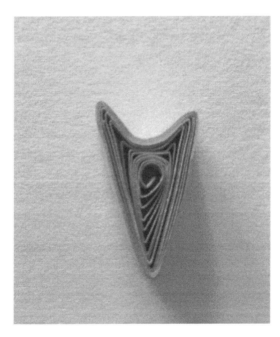

Release the tool and smooth the curve out with your fingers to shape.

Arrowhead

Beginning with a teardrop shape, hold the pointed end in your non-dominant hand and pinch the base end into a tight point.

Without letting go, slide your fingers down to meet the fingers of your opposite hand to create the side angles

Heart

Once again, begin with a teardrop. Press in the shape's base by using the point of your quilling tool to make a small indentation.

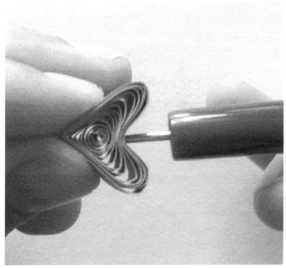

Release the tool and carefully press in each side of the heart to complete the center crease.

44

Pentagon and Star

To make a pentagon, first, create an elongated semi-circle, as shown above.

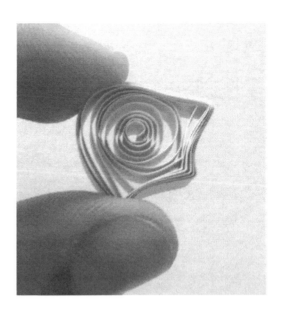

Pinch the center of the flat side using the same method you used when making the tulip shape; this is the peak of your pentagon.

Keeping the peak in the center, square off the bottom with two equal pinches on either side.

To turn the pentagon into a star, press inward on each flat surface with your fingers or a quilling tool and then further refine each angle into peaks.

Holly Leaf

This shape is far and away from the most difficult to create. For sanity's sake, you'll want to become comfortable making all of the other shapes before attempting this one!

Begin by making a marquis. Insert a set of tweezers into the shape; try to grip only about a third of the inside coil.

Keeping the grip with your tweezers, turn the marquis as needed and pinch a small point on either side of each peak.

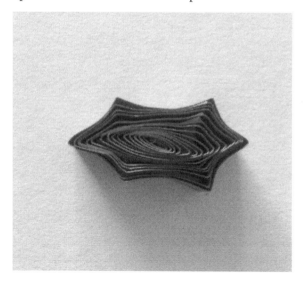

You could also make the holly leaf by first making a square, adding a point to each end, and then shaping all the angles into peaks. I find the tweezer method easier, but try both ways to see which gives you better results.

Chapter 3: Tools and Material

Some have kits, some have drawers, and some have an entire room dedicated to their art and craft supplies. It is best to start quilling with a kit. While it is satisfying to hoard materials, you might end up feeling distracted and overwhelmed by the number of paper strips and tools at your disposal—Master a few tools and the basic techniques first before trying out more materials.

Quilling kits for beginners are readily available in many online quilling supply stores. Most of the kits contain a pack of precut quilling paper and a slotted tool. Some have boards and combs. Many kits also have non-specialty tools (Think of glue, tweezers, and pins).

If you want to fill your quilling kit, you must prepare your own storage box first. You can either buy or improvise. Next, you should shop online for specialty tools. Visit your school supply store for the basic art and craft supplies. Also, search your home for some alternative and additional shaping tools.

Specialty Tools

Specialty tools are made specifically for art—in this case, quilling. They are designed in such a way that they provide convenience to a craft-maker. Right now, some tools are labeled according to the level of expertise of the intended users. You should pick tools that are tagged for beginners. Below are the quilling tools that you should know.

Slotted Tool

The slotted tool is the best friend of every beginner in quilling. This is primarily for making coils. It has two parts: the handle and the needle. The needle part is metal, at least 1/2-inch long, and has a slit where you will place the tip of your paper strip. The said slit makes rolling easier, but it leaves a tiny crimp in the middle of your paper. Its handle may be made from plastic or wood. Most slotted tools have a cylindrical handle. Some may be etched or molded differently. The length of the handle and needles varies from one model to another.

Needle Tool

The needle tool, also known as the needle form, is also intended for making coils. Unlike the slotted tool, though, this one does not have a slit in its needle part, which results in a crimp-less coil. It is best to master the slotted tool first, followed by the needle tool, and then the quilling comb.

Quilling Coach

Quilling coach is a flat plastic board made to help keep the paper strips in place as you roll it using the slotted tool. It is also used to ensure that the edges of your coils are even. This tool has a circular head and a handle. Its head features circles of different sizes and a hole in the middle where you can insert the slotted tool's needle. Most quilling coaches are made from either colored or transparent plastic.

Circle Sizer/Mold Board

A circle sizer is also intended to help you make coils of the same size. Unlike a quilling coach, though, you need to remove your rolled paper strip from the needle tool and then place it on the circle sizer. There are two types of circle sizer: the ruler type and the board type. The ruler type, which may be made from plastic, looks like a typical ruler but bigger and with circular holes of different sizes in the middle part. You are going to put your rolled paper strips in the holes. The board type may be made from either plastic or wood. Aside from circles, the board type may feature molding holes for square, triangle, heart, oval, leaf and other shapes. This one is sometimes referred to as the quilling moldboard.

Quilling Comb

A quilling comb, also known as an onion holder, looks like the one you use for your hair, except that the metallic teeth are longer and the handle is shorter in the former. Compared to the slotted tool, you can form various shapes and patterns with this instrument.

Crimper Tool

As its name suggests, the crimper tool helps you make uniformly crimped paper strips. This is a great time and energy saver as you do not need to fold the paper strips by hand alone.

Quilling Border Buddy

The slotted tool can only help in making circular coils. A quilling border buddy is an answer to the slotted tool's limitation. You can mold your paper strips with the quilling border buddy to form squares or triangles of different sizes. You can also make bigger circles with this tool.

Additionally, you may use this to make borders, which you can fill with smaller paper rings later on. This tool is either wood- or plastic-made.

There are other specialty tools made for quilling, but most of them are for molding. You can opt for the more complex molders later. For now, you should try alternatives molders that you can easily find in your home.

Alternatives

Resourcefulness is one of the attributes of every craft-maker. Apart from cutting their quilling paper strips, some quillers go as far as making their versions of the slotted tool. You do not have to do that. However, it pays to use the alternatives as you wait for your slotted tool and precut quilling paper to arrive. Or, you may also use them alongside the specialty tools to form rings of different sizes.

Toothpicks

The diameter of a standard toothpick is close to that of a slotted tool's needle. Toothpicks are quite easy to break, but practicing your rolls with them can help you learn how to gently roll your paper strips.

Pencils and Pens

Using pencils and pens for your rolls will leave behind noticeable holes in your paper coils. This does not have to be a drawback. You can mix and match coils whose holes are of different sizes for your artworks.

Knitting Needles

The use of knitting needles as an alternative quilling tool is similar to that of pencils and pens. Knitting needles are just a bit lighter. However, if no one likes knitting in your home, finding these tools entails additional work. You should just focus on things that are readily available in your house.

Combs

Your regular combs will work fine as quilling combs. Get some of the combs you rarely use but still look neat. Wash and brush them first before you use them for quilling. Once you decide to use them for quilling, do not reuse them for combing your hair.

Lids

Small lids can serve as additional tools to a quilling border buddy. You can scour your kitchen for old bottles and jars. Get the lids, wash them, and leave them to dry. You can wrap your paper strips around a lid to mold them.

Bottles, containers, chopsticks, or even woodblocks may be used for molding and making coils. Just remember to clean or smoothen the items you intend to use for quilling. You do not want to stain your paper strips with sauces from the old bottles, do you?

Basics

Quilling is not just about shaping paper strips. It also involves other steps, such as measuring, tracing, cutting, gluing, and pinching. For the other steps, you should include pencils and rulers, as well as the following supplies in your quilling kit:

Cutting Tools

Besides investing in good scissors exclusive for quilling, it pays to have a sharp cutter and a self-healing mat. You should add a thread snipper in your kit as well. Although a thread snipper is mainly used for sewing, it can also cut paper quickly and comfortably. It also pays to have a cuticle nipper in your kit as you can use it to cut some uneven parts in your quilled paper strips. Additionally, you may use it to get rid of visible dried glue.

Adhesives

Forget the glue gun for quilling. Needle-tip craft glue is more appropriate. The heat from a glue gun may damage your quilling paper. With craft glue, there would be not much of a problem. Another advantage of this adhesive is its narrow opening, which results in easy application to thin paper strips.

Tweezers

Have at least two pairs of tweezers in your quilling kit. This will help you hold your coils without unraveling or warping them and place your delicate paper strips into narrow spaces.

Pins and Tacks

You can have different pins in your quilling kit. You may choose from the following type: glass headpins, plastic headpins, ballpoint pins, eye pins, silk pins, quilting pins, and T pins. You will use the pins as guards to your paper coils to prevent them from unraveling on the board. You may also use a pin to unclog your needle-tip craft glue. Have a box of tacks as well.

Board

Boards are for the background of some quilled artworks. You are going to use corkboards for practices as well. In the meantime, you may resort to cardboard. Invest in sturdier boards once you have mastered the basics of quilling. Some quilled projects call for additional tools and supplies. Nevertheless, the abovementioned materials are the things you are most likely to work on within most of your practices and projects. Do not forget to experiment with some of the home objects that you may use for rolling and molding.

Chapter 4: Quilling Basics and Tips for Beginners

As a beginner quilter or even as an expert/professional whose interest is to survive in the craft of quilling without much stress, here are few tips that could help you actualize this. They include.

Using a Background Platform that is Colored

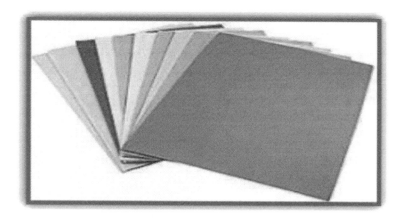

If you use a quilling background, attractively laden with colors, it will help boost the sight impression and improve your craftwork's attention after completion and while on display. If the kind of background paper you are using is void of color or colors, say a plain white sheet, you can easily give the paper any color of your choice, and that's it; you've just made one for yourself.

Use Paper Strip (Shredder)

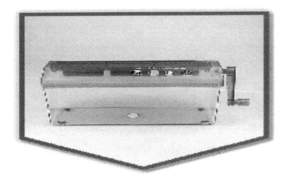

A shredder in paper quilling is a box-like tool normally made of plastic materials with a winding handle. The paper to be threaded is placed neatly in the opened allowable part of the box, and the handle is wind. It is the manual paper stripping method.

Using the scissors to do your quilling process could be cumbersome and tiring sometimes. Subsequently, it is suggested that you opt for the thread sniper or slicer. In this way, you save some time and get near-perfect quilled paperwork free from glue attachments.

However, it is not to say that the scissors aren't a good companion in this business. The scissor can still be effectively used in the absence of any other better alternative.

Use the Needle Before the Comb

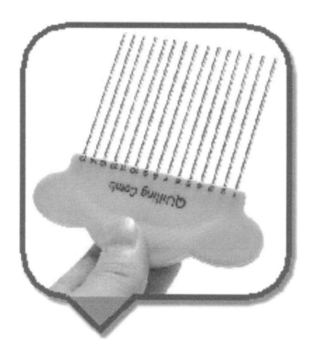

In this craft, the experience pays quite a lot! Some persons find the quilling comb quite difficult to use in the first place. Using the quilling needle tool first before applying the quilling comb would help save a lot, both time and energy, and help keep the middle of your rolled coil in check.

Learn to Roll Two Strips Together

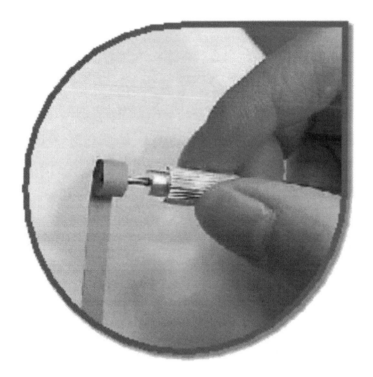

As you continue to grow in this craft experience, you will come to discover that rolling up just a single paper strip could lead to weariness. Still, it is advisable for you and the strip to always join at least two strips together before taking a manual hand roll.

Get a Quilling Sponge

The quilling sponge is more or less like a holding container that helps to hold the glue bottle while working. It is to prevent unsolicited glue/gum spillage on a given job or project, as the glue bottle or container is normally placed or turned with its tip facing downwards on the sponge for easy access and quick application. The sponge also serves as a tool for cleaning up unwanted glue. Particularly those that are on the fingers and palms, in addition to spillovers, if any.

Rolling Using a Slotted Tool

This technique lets you create coils out of your quilling paper strips. Coils are present in most quilt creations, so it only fits to know how to make them. To learn how to roll properly, grab a paper strip and your slotted tool. Keep your needle-tip craft glue nearby and follow the steps below:

1. Hold the slotted tool using your dominant hand while the paper strip is in your other hand.
2. Insert the tip of your paper strip into the slit of your slotted tool's needle.
3. Hold the paper strip with your non-dominant hand's thumb and index finger.
4. Start rolling the slotted tool. It is the right way. Do not wrap the paper strip around the slotted tool's needle.
5. You may roll the paper strip up to the very end or leave something like a tail.

There are three types of coils you can create with the steps mentioned above. These are: open, closed and tight.

- To make an open coil, gently remove the rolled paper strip from the slotted tool and put it down right away.
- To make a closed coil, gently remove the rolled paper strip from the slotted tool, let it loosen but apply a small amount of glue at the end of the paper strip.

- To make a tight coil, gently remove the rolled paper strip from the slotted tool and hold it lightly for 20 seconds. Apply glue at the end of the paper strip.

If you want your coils to be of similar size, make sure that the paper strips you use are also of the same size. Additionally, use your circle sizer ruler or board to measure your coils.

Create as many coils as you can until you master rolling with your slotted tool. Do not throw your coils right away, though. No matter how displeasing they might seem, you can use them to try forming the basic shapes and learning how to insert small coils into big ones later.

You'd be surprised that you can master this technique in an hour or two. You should be warned, though. Rolling paper strips continuously may lead to cramps. To prevent this, relax your grip on your slotted tool and paper strip. Stretch and let your fingers rest every so often. You might want to consider holding a cloth or padding between your dominant hand and the slotted tool.

Rolling Using a Needle Tool, Toothpick, or Any Other Alternative

Rolling using a needle tool, toothpick, or any other alternative to the slotted tool is a little bit harder because of the lack of slit where you can place one end of your paper strip. Although tricky, this technique does not leave behind a crimp in the middle of your coil, which usually happens when you use the slotted tool.

To start, keep your fingers a little bit moist and follow the steps below:

1. Use your dominant hand to hold your tool while your other hand is for the paper strip. You may add a quilling coach to your needle tool.
2. Curve the end of the paper strip around your tool. Do this near the tip of the tool for easy and speedy removal of coils later.
3. Gently press the end of the paper strip attached to your tool to keep it in place.
4. Start rolling your tool.

To create the three types of coils using a needle tool, toothpick, or any other alternative, follow through the same steps as those mentioned for rolling with a slotted tool. When you are done mastering the art of making coils, go to a whole new level by transforming your coils into basic quilling shapes. You can do this by hand alone. The following are some of the basic quilling shapes you can create with your paper coils.

Practice making basic shapes as many times as you want. Experiment with wider and narrower paper strips, as well as with longer and shorter paper strips. You can also try modifying the techniques bit by bit

Teardrop

To make a teardrop-shaped paper strip, pinch one part of your coil. Apply glue at the end.

Eye

Pinch two opposite ends of your coil. Make sure they are equally molded on each side. Glue the loose end of your coil.

Leaf

The leaf-shaped coil is similar to the eye. You also have to pinch two opposite parts of your coil. After that, push the pinched parts towards each other. Do not forget to apply glue at the other end.

Petal

To create a petal-shaped coil, you should also pinch two opposite parts of your coil. However, one of the pinched parts should be bigger than the other.

Practice making these basic shapes as many times as you want. Experiment with wider and narrower paper strips, as well as with longer and shorter paper strips. You can also try modifying the techniques bit by bit.

Rolling Using a Border Buddy or Any of Its Alternatives

Some quilling border buddies have handles, so learning how to use them is easier. However, some do not have any handle at all. You have no other option but to hold the body of the border buddy. But this could be an advantage. You will be trained to use the border buddy and lids, small bottles, or any other item used as a molder.

The steps for rolling a paper strip using a border buddy or any of its alternatives are similar to rolling using a needle tool unless your molder is not round, oblong, or oval. Always start with round border buddies. Try creating big coils of different sizes. Once you are done with the round ones, proceed with the triangle and square border buddies. When you use a lid, make sure your paper strip is narrower. Otherwise, you will lead up with a coil full of crimps on the edges. Below are the steps in using a border buddy or any other molder for that matter:

1. Use your dominant hand to hold the molder while the other hand is for your paper strip.
2. Put one end of your paper strip into the molder. Press it with your thumb to keep it in place.
3. Start twisting your molder slowly but guide your paper strip using your non-dominant hand's thumb and index finger. If your molder has one or more corners, press your paper strip in those corners.
4. After the first roll, apply glue to the end of your paper strip that is affixed to your molder.
5. Continue rolling until you achieve your desired thickness. You may or may not leave something like the tail of your coil.

If you are going to make a closed coil, do not remove your paper strip from the molder right away. Apply glue at the other end of your paper strip while it is still on the molder. After that, remove your paper strip and hold it for 20 seconds (or until the glued end is not likely to slide) to maintain its shape.

Create coils of different colors, shapes, sizes, widths, and lengths. Try out various plastic and glass bottles, jars, and other containers. Use wood blocks to make big squares, rectangles, or triangles. You may transform your coils into other shapes by pinching them or just leave them as they are.

Gluing Coils Together

Gluing coils are made easy and less messy with needle-tip craft glue. But for your practices, it might be a waste to use such glue right away. As an alternative, you may use regular glue and a pin.

You are going to use the glue to join coils together. For now, you can glue the different coils you just created. Do not obsess about forming patterns in the meantime. Below are the steps in applying regular glue using a pin.

1. Prepare your tweezers, cuticle nipper, and a piece of scrap paper.
2. Squeeze a little amount of glue to the piece of paper. Close your glue to keep it from drying.
3. After that, get a bit of glue using your pin and spread it to one side of the coil. You may use your hands to hold big coils, but you should use tweezers for the small ones.
4. Get another coil and affix it to the glued part of one coil. Hold it together for at least 20 seconds or until the glue dries.

Practice gluing coils that are of the same width. Use your cuticle nipper to get rid of dried glue or to cut some uneven parts.

Gluing Coils on a Medium

One of the simplest quilled artworks you can make is card designs. You do not need to glue coils together for this. You can attach the coils directly to your card or any other medium. For this, you need to put a small amount of glue at the bottom of your coils and glue it to paper. Try gluing coils of different shapes individually. After that, try to put coils together. To do this, follow the steps for gluing coils together first. Apply glue to the bottom of your adjoined coils and affix it to your paper.

Inserting Small Coils into Big Coils

One of the toughest steps in creating a quilled artwork is inserting small coils into big ones. To help you stay sane throughout the entire process, get your two tweezers and a handkerchief for your sweaty hands. Prepare your big coils and small coils as well. Below are the steps in inserting small coils:

1. Glue your big coils on paper. Do not worry about forming figures or patterns for now. Just glue them.
2. Next, apply glue to the bottom and sides of your small coils.
3. After that, use your tweezers to insert the small coils to fill up the big coils' holes. Start inserting the slightly bigger ones first.
4. If there are some noticeable spaces left, make small coils that can fit into those. You may cut the coils you already need to form the small coils.

For the loose and open coils, you can place them beside the big coils. Put a paste to the bottom and sides of the coils. These are going to be linked to the other coils. It is quite tedious to apply glue to the bottom of loose coils, especially if they have tails.

Here is an important reminder when applying glue: It is better to apply a little more than a little less. If you apply a too small amount, your coil may get detached easily. If you apply a little more, you can simply remove the excess dried glue with a cuticle nipper or a pin. A pin works best for the dried glue in the inner parts of the coil. If it is quite difficult to reach, though, it is better to leave the dried glue in peace.

Using a Quilling Comb

There are plenty of elaborate coils you can make with the quilling comb. However, this tool is also complicated to use. You are going to combine weaving and looping when you use the quilling comb. Below are some of the basic shapes you can make with a quilling comb.

Petal

With the quilling comb, you can make paper petals without pinching your coils. There are many petal designs you can form with the quilling comb but below are the steps to make it easier.

- Hold your paper strip using your dominant hand while the quilling comb is at your other hand.
- Fold a tiny part at the end of the paper strip to create a hook.
- Place your paper strip at the back of the quilling comb. Hook it at the bottommost tine of the quilling comb. The tiny folded part should be at the front.
- Pull the other end of the paper strip to the front on the second tine of the quilling comb.
- Apply glue to the tiny folded part of the paper strip.
- Fold the long end of the paper strip and glue it to its tiny folded part. Press it gently.
- Pull the long end to the back of the paper strip again.
- Weave the paper strip to the front on the third tine of the quilling comb.
- Pull the long end down and then fold it to the back of the quilling comb again. Apply glue to the part where the hook was once located.

- Repeat the same steps to the succeeding tines of your quilling comb.
- Keep on looping until the end of your paper strip. If there is an excess, cut it using a thread snipper.

Just like making coils with the slotted tool, you may simply remove your paper strip and let it loosen. You may or may not glue its other end. If you want it to be a tight coil, hold the two ends for at least 20 seconds and then apply glue at the end. Or, you may just hold the one end where the hook was and let the other end loosen.

Chapter 5: Practical Tips to Make Projects Faster

Paper quilling is madly cool, however, in case you're an apprentice, the expectation to absorb information can be steep. Fortunately, knowing a couple of crucial tips and hacks has a significant effect.

Utilize Beautiful Foundations

A prominent white foundation can be diverting and point out every blemish, while a shaded foundation offers marginally less complexity to your quilled shapes and is substantially more sympathetic. It'll assist watchers with seeing precisely what you need them to concentrate on the general perfection of your design.

Pick String Snippers Over Scissors

Picking the correct paper quilling devices is significant, and cumbersome scissors are not your companion in this sensitive art. You're in an ideal situation with a lightweight pair of string snippers. They're suitable for clipping off the glue-bound parts of the snips, and their little size causes them to fit excellently into any quilling tool compartment.

Get an Ideal Center Coiling in Each of Your Coiling

You needn't bother with a needle device to make a flawless coil. Whenever utilized the correct way, an opened equipment can give you the round focus you need without creasing.

73

One stunt is to continue turning your quilling instrument after you've arrived at the finish of your strip until you feel the device give way. The device tears the little bit of paper that would've been the crease, leaving you with an ideal curl. On the off chance that your quilling device can't confront this sort of turning, you can likewise use a pin or penetrating device to streamline the pleat a while later.

Tear as Opposed to Clipping

Yes, you need to make clean lines and shroud all the creases in your shapes at whatever point conceivable. Be that as it may, now and then there's no place to stow away. On the off chance that you don't care for the vibe of sharp paper creases, you can tear the finish of your quilling strip as opposed to clipping it with scissors. That way, the join will have a milder impact.

Move With, Not Against, the Edge of the Quilling Strip

When quilling paper gets cut, the sharp edge cuts it from above in a descending movement. This makes both of the long sides roll somewhat descending. The impact is insignificant to such an extent that it's difficult to see with the naked eye, yet you can feel it when you run the strip between your fingers. For a progressively flawless curl, move with the bend (the descending arch should look down). It may be somewhat dubious to do this on your initial attempts, and avoiding this progression won't hurt the manner in which your quilled look. Be that as it may, when you begin focusing, doing it alongside these lines turns out to be practically instinctual.

Utilize a Needle Structure Before a Quilling Brush or Comb

Quilling brushes or comb can appear to be difficult and tedious to use. You may feel like they're not worth the effort, however, attempt this tip before you abandon them: first, roll a little curl using a quilling needle tool. At that point, move the coil to your quilling brush and make your shape. This technique needle structure first, quilling brush after should help keep the focal point of your loop set up (and your mental stability flawless).

Bend over Your Strips for a Grippy Roll

At the point when you're rolling an additional enormous curl, the middle will as a rule, end up breaking liberated from the quilling instrument before you're finished. All you can do by then is to roll the rest by hand. In any case, you can stay away from all that by bending over the strip to begin your curl: the twofold thickness will keep everything where it has a place. To do this, you can either overlay your first strip over, or use two pieces on one another.

Use Nippers to Fix Your Errors

No one's ideal, and regardless of how exactly you are in your work, pretty much every project will undoubtedly have a little blooper someplace. That is where fingernail skin nippers come in. Accessible in any drugstore in the nail care passageway, nippers will let you effectively cut off a lopsided edge or expel undesirable glue after it's dry.

Prepare Your Wipe

A wipe is a quiller's closest companion, and an arrangement is charming. The holder holds your needle-tip stick bottle topsy-turvy so it's all set whenever you need it, while the wet wipe shields your glue from drying out and stopping up the tip. You can likewise use the outside of the wipe to clean any adhesive that gets onto your fingers.

To make your own, simply cut a kitchen wipe and put it inside a little bowl or ramekin. You can even make an arrangement that is sufficiently smaller to fit inside your quilling unit.

Be Companion with Your Eye Pin

So, you left your top off and now your needle tip is stopped up. It's alright, you presumably didn't think about our wipe stunt yet. Be that as it may, there's still expectation! With an eye pin, you can unplug the tip and return to making your specialty. The eye pin's dull end makes it a more secure alternative than a sewing pin. Simply abstain from leaving the eye pin in the tip for quite a while, since the bolt can rust and stain your glued design.

Chapter 6: Cards (Pretty Flowers; Asian Inspiration; Butterflies and Blossoms)

Greeting Cards

Step 1: Normally, for some kind of quilling patterns, you will need to do some sketching, and to do this, you will need a pencil and paper (canvas) if you have one. It's best to sketch on a firm piece of cardboard paper or a paper with a desirable thickness level.

Your sketch could be anything, a house, a flower, a bicycle or car bird, a tree, or anything that comes to your mind.

Step 2: The most fundamental shapes in quilling originate from making circles or curls and squeezing them into wanted shapes.

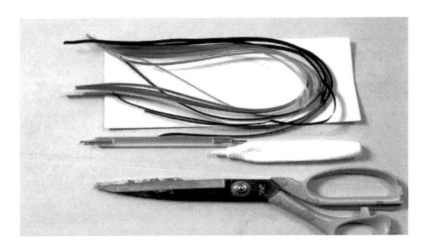

If your ideal blossom sketch needs a leaf-like teardrop shape, simply squeeze one side of the loop, and you will be amazed that you can shape any style by yourself by squeezing, pleating and sticking cycles. Be allowed to explore! Having done the previously mentioned projects above, follow the subsequent stages constantly to finish up.

Step 3:Put a small amount of gum/glue to your shapes at their various points of interfacing with the end edge part of the strip(s) as well as at joinery points. Always prepare your shapes over your sketches and apply a little pressure while waiting for the glue to harden.

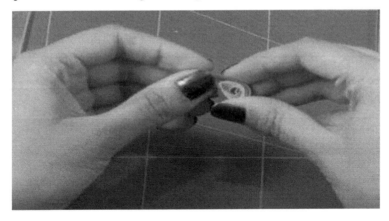

Step 4: From a variety of paper strips, get/pick for yourself one strip and coil the paper around the tip of the quilling tool, which in this case, is the slotted tool.

Step 5: Having done the above, gently pull the coiled strip off the slotted tool.

Then shaped your coil to the exact size you desire and then apply a small drop of glue to the end tail of the paper strip to close you to finish the coiling process.

Step 6: Take any size of colored paper as in your predetermined color and quilting design. Ensure the paper you can use for this background has a considerable gram in thickness.

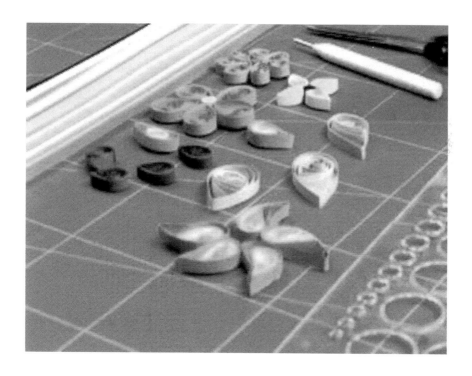

If you can lay your hands on a desirable colored A4 paper, then you are good to go. But if not, you can also get a paper of any length wideness and cut or trim to any size of your choice, then fold it in half to make the card of hard-back.

Step 7: This part entails the design and decoration of your card. The first type of design to be considered is to try and achieve the rose-like pattern of design by making small cuts on the quilling paper. Then, roll it on the slotted tool and pinching/bending the coil's edges outside to give it that shape of a rose.

You can even join more than one quilling paper to give your card that whimsical and alluring look that everybody might want. Make the same number of coils as you need with various shapes and sizes, utilizing the opened instrument, tweezers device, pleating device, pins, stick, and the whole quilling device is important.

Fix all the objects of different styles and shapes on the front cover and the card's back. Generally, the front of the card keeps more of the quilled shapes and designs. Make your arrangement to be in a specific pattern, or randomly place them depending on the design you intend to make or create.

From experience, it is always better you sketch your predetermined design faintly on your paper cover front for easy object placement, or you could choose to do the sketching on another paper sheet so to serve as a guide.

81

Don't forget to create a space for some write up. Or you can do your major write-up on the inside of the already-made card. It is either writing directly on it or by attaching a paper-leave on the inside of the card to write on.

Quilled Letters

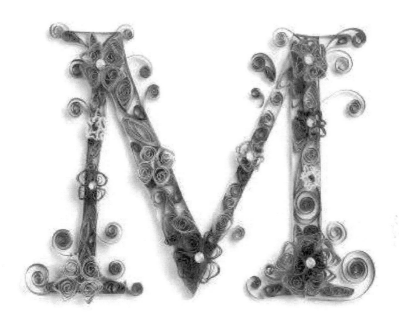

Quilled artworks featuring one letter are one of the most sought-after designs. It is called monogram quilling. When you look at them closely, though, you may get intimidated by the number and intricacy of the straight and curve lines required to form the letters. Don't worry. This project is not that hard to make.

Materials:

- Precut quilling paper or self-made cardstock paper strips of the same width
- Board with white background
- A printed copy of any letter you want to make (the outline of the letter will do)

- Sharp pencil
- Craft glue
- Two tweezers
- Pins
- Scissors or thread snapper
- Cuticle nipper

Steps:

1. Place the printed copy of the letter you want to make on the board.
2. Using your sharp pencil, trace the outline of the letter.
3. Make the different coils you want to add to your artwork.
4. Trace the slightly etched outline of the letter using your preferred paper strip. It will stand out from all of your artwork, so choose a color that looks bright and different from the ones you use for your coils.
5. Fold and curl your paper strip as needed. Attach a paper strip of the same color to cover the entire outline of the letter.
6. Use pins but keep them at least 1 inch apart.
7. Next, glue your paper strip into the board.
8. Leave it to dry. While you wait, plan the coils you will insert in the letter and the coils for its sides and edges. You may also consider adding some wavy lines.
9. Cut the uneven parts of your outline with a cuticle nipper. Get rid of some visible dried glue as well.

Place the bigger coils inside the outline of your letter. Apply glue to the sides and bottom of your coils. You can insert them by hand. Use the tweezers to adjust their placement.

Next, insert the small coils inside. Apply glue to their sides and bottom as well. Use tweezers to put them in.

Add some open coils with tails on the sides of your letter. Glue them properly. Leave it to dry.

Remove the visible dried glue.

Are you satisfied with your artwork? Consider displaying it as wall decor. Has it framed to keep dust at bay?

Try the steps herein to make different letters and numbers as well. You can use your creations as decors for parties.

You may also draw the letters and numbers yourself. You may even draw landscapes, seascapes, silhouettes of people, or outlines of simple items. Find inspiration in your surroundings. You can certainly find one that you can use for your quilling artwork.

Birthday Card

Ribbon:

Make two bunny ears and two arrowheads, using full-length grape purple strips. Wrap the center of the ribbon with a 1/8" (3 mm) wide strip.

Lavender Marquise Flower and Flower Buds:

Make four flowers for each flower. Roll three marquises, using 1/6 length lavender strips. Make six more marquises for buds.

Lavender Tight Coil Flower Buds:

Make four tight coils using 1/8 lavender strips.

Leaves:

Make fourteen large and six small leaves. For each leaf, make three-loop vertical husking, using moss green strips. Make four more leaves. For each leaf, make two-loop vertical husking.

Vines:

Make six loose scrolls with ¼ length yellow-green strips and two more with 1/6 length yellow-green strips.

Pollen:

Make six tight coils, using 1/16 length canary yellow strips.

Heart-Shaped Stem:

Fold one (21 cm) long moss green strip in half and curve the ends inward. Glue the ends at the same time to form a heart shape.

Assembly:

1. Glue the heart-shaped stem in the center of the card.
2. Glue the large leaves outside the bottom of the heart-shaped stem and glue the small leaves above them.

3. Glue the lavender marquise flowers outside the heart stem and between the leaves. Glue the vines on the inside of the heart shape.
4. Glue the pollen between the flowers and leaves. Add the ribbon in the center of the heart shape.
5. Add a happy birthday to the center of the card.

Simple Flowers

Another simple flower is a cornflower.

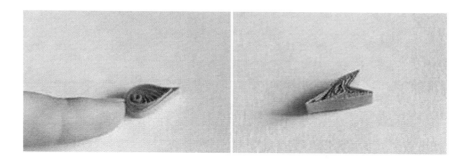

Imagine how delicate it is to get a handmade New Year card with a daisy applied to it! And you can make such a bouquet in an hour.

Instructions:

1. Cut out 8mm-wide and 20cm-long white paper strips.
2. Twist them with a drop.
3. Cut an 8mm-wide and 20 cm-long strip from yellow paper.
4. Make a closed coil.
5. Glue the elements—the chamomile is ready.
6. We should focus separately on creating volumetric colors. For your base, you need a special cardboard cone.

Water lily looks no less original and beautiful on crafts (especially in applications on notebooks). It also needs a cardboard floor.

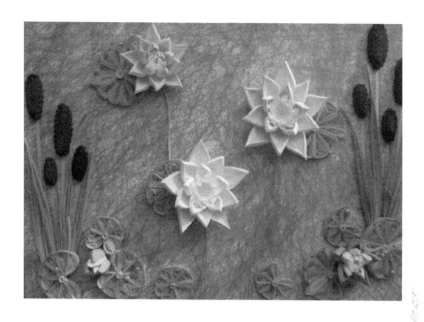

Instructions:

1. We make 14 drops.
2. Glue 8 blanks onto the edge of the base cone.
3. We glue another five drops to the second stage.
4. The last element is defined in the middle. The water lily is ready.

Simple Heart

Overlay the strip at half, twist one end and then, roll freely by hand until you have made one portion of a heart. Repeat this process on the opposite end, rolling the strip the other way. For this quilling card, you will need:

- Strips of paper
- Cocktail stick
- PVA glue

Butterfly

Art is naturally appealing, and paper quills butterfly is an art. Therefore, paper quills butterfly is appealing to not just the eye, but the mind. However, there seems to be something that ignites a deeper sense of artistic elegance in paper quills butterflies.

If you know how to make paper quills butterfly, you sure would be among the finest artists in the world. Wouldn't you love to be a rewarded fine artist? I see you want to. Now, I will introduce you to the basics and equally expose the secret things that could make your paper quills butterfly unique.

Required Materials for Paper Quills Butterfly:

To arrive at a decent paper quills butterfly, there are a few materials to put in place.

The basic five materials include:

- The quilling paper
- Quilling pins
- Quilling stencil
- Slotted quilling tool
- Dispensing quilling glue

If you do not own any of the tools above, the chances of arriving at something elegant would be quite low. Some persons substitute for other papery materials as a replacement for the traditional quilling paper. But then, the result would either be a distorted finishing or a swaying design.

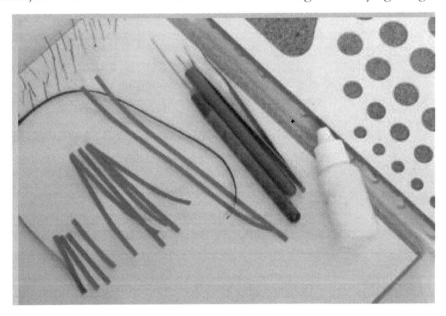

How to Make Paper Quill Butterflies:

Gather the Required Supplies.

For a small butterfly, the required supplies include:

- (4) 1 ½-inch strips
- (6) 3-inch strips
- (2) 6-inch strips
- A 12-inch strip of black slotted quilling tool glue

Optional Tools:

- Needle tool
- Tweezers
- Circle sizing board
- Corkboard and pins

Fold the Strips in the Corkboard:

After you have the mentioned tools in place, punch holes on the corkboard. The hole may not necessarily have to be like what you have in this photo. You may design however way you desire. In this photo, a pink strip is used because it is what I choose. There are more lovely colors, and if you do not mind, I will recommend some colors for you. You may go for something like royal blue, pitch color, or emerald green; if you love pink, no problem.

Arrange the Strips as Shown Here:

At this point, take a studying look at the image above. You can see the looks of the quills. Now, here is how to achieve the design. I believe you have the glue with you because it is needed now. Just as in the picture above, arrange each pink (depending on the color you are using) strip to look the same. Once you have been able to do so, apply the quilling glue, and try not to hold the bottom of the strap tight. Since it may be difficult not to hold it while applying the glue, hold it with less pressure so that each wing is pointy when the glue is dry.

Rose

It is easiest for beginners to sort out schemes with descriptions of the quilling roses, so recommend artisans.

Instructions:

1. Cut out a 20cm-long and 10mm-wide paper strip.

2. Insert the end of the strip into the eye and wrap it three times around the axis.

3. Apply the adhesive with a toothpick and lay the tape at the right angles to you.

4. Make another round with a bell on the needle and drip the glue again.

5. If you repeat steps 3 and 4, place the entire strip. Rose is done.

Chapter 7: Jewelry (Diamond and Double Flower; Silver and Gold Earrings)

Double Flower Finger Ring

Paper quilled flower finger rings are adorable pieces of art. Interestingly; they are easy to make.

1. Join at least 4 quilling paper strips of the same color together to form a long paper strip.
2. Create a 12mm-coil fold from the long paper strip.
3. Make fringes from paper strips using scissors. The paper strip color should be the same unless you wish to use a different color.
4. Curl the fringed strips on the external coil fold and press it firmly to achieve a firmer flower shape—clear varnish by applying a coat to the fringed paper strips and allow to dry.
5. Use craft glue to attach the ornate flower to the ring.

Behold, you have one of the few most beautiful ring arts out there in your palms. Create more until you become a perfect crafter.

Diamond Rose Quilling

Materials Required:

- Quilling paper—any width will work, however, 3/8 inch or 1/4 inch are used most normally. Both are accessible as standard sizes or cut your own strips. Around a 7-inch length makes a decent, full rose

- Quilling instrument—opened device or needle device (I'll use a standard opened equipment for this instructional exercise)

- Scissors

- Paste—I like to use a reasonable gel; likewise, Scotch Glue

- Plastic cover—use as paste palette

- Paper penetrating device, T-pin, or round toothpick—to apply stick

Directions:

1. Cut a segment of 3/8-inch x 7-inches paper.

2. Slip one end of the strip into an opened device from the left. It doesn't make a difference whether you are right or left-handed, as both will have assignments.

3. Hold the instrument vertically in your right hand, the strip in your left, and start to roll the device toward the left. Make a couple of unrests to make sure about the paper and structure the focal point of the rose.

4. Utilize your left hand to twist the strip straight up at a 90-degree point. There's no compelling reason to wrinkle the overlay.

5. Keep rolling the instrument toward the left, turning over the crease as you go. Simultaneously, use your left hand to bit-by-bit carry the strip down to a flat position. I understand this sound ungainly, yet attempt it—you'll before long observe it turns into a smooth collapsing and moving activity.

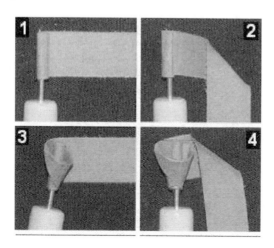

Next, the left hand is bringing down the strip; the right hand is still rolling the device. Now it's an ideal opportunity to overlap and go once more.

Tip: Make another overlap right when you've wrapped up the past one.

The second crease/roll has been finished.

6. Repeat the moving/collapsing the same number of times as it takes to go through the strip—it's just as simple as that.

    Look, a rose is coming to fruition! This is after six or seven folds... notice it's shaping topsy-turvy and would make a decent bud at this stage.

7. At the point when near the end of the strip, detach any overabundance, slip the rose off the device, and allow the folds to unwind. Shape the rose by tenderly turning or untwisting the folds of a piece. Conceal the torn end of the strip by sticking it to the underside of the rose.

    Tip: A torn paper end will be less perceptible when stuck because it mixes superior to a sharp cut. Smooth out the middle crease brought about by the opened device by embeddings and turning the tip of a paper penetrating device or round toothpick.

Quilling Jewelry

Paper quilling jewelry is as old as ages. Today, a large part of the world is practicing the unique art of quilling jewelry, and it's now a trend. From the look of things, diamonds, golds, and silvers may soon lose their relevance to paper-quilled jewelry in the industry. You can make the most exceptional jewelry from paper quilling within some dedicated minutes. It is a matter of paper strips, glue and a few other tools.

Materials Required for Quilling Jewelry:

- Quilling paper strips of varying colors
- Quilling comb
- Slotted quilling tool
- Crimper tool
- Mini mold
- X-acto knife
- Jump ring
- Glue
- Quilling board
- Tweezers
- Plier

Paper Quilled Necklace

a. Create 7 paper strips of varying colors into 7 large petals with more full loops and pinch them into teardrop folds.

b. Fold 2 paper strips of another color into closed coil folds using a slotted quilling tool.

c. Glue the folds to the internal points of 2 outer petals.

d. You need to make the inner petals by creating 5 open coil folds and pinching one end of each to make a teardrop fold.

e. Glue in the inner petals inside the larger leaves.

f. Make a large coil fold and smaller coil folds, as in the picture above.

g. Insert the large coil fold in the middle of the design.

h. Use tweezers to place the smaller coil folds between the sizeable open coil folds and glue them together.

i. Play around with the arrangement of the folds in the larger folds until it's satisfactory. Glue the folds together and allow them to dry.

j. Attach the necklace fastening to make the quilled necklace wearable. You may apply a sealant to keep the jewelry safe from exposure to water.

Silver-and-Gold Teardrop Earring

Silver Teardrop Earring:

It is effortless to make a beautiful silver earring. This guide walks you through making a paper-quilled teardrop earring seamlessly.

1. In this tutorial, I am using just two colors—light and dark silver. Pick your paper strip color according to preference. Moreover, you need 10 paper strips—5 light silver and 5 silver. Make each paper strip into a closed coil fold—more substantial and smaller coil folds.
2. Pinch one end of each coil fold to make a teardrop fold.
3. Wrap another color of the paper strip on each paper strips; repeat the process for all 5 folds.
4. Attach 2 teardrop folds in pairs to form a heart shape. You should have 5 teardrop folds—two heart shapes and one teardrop fold.

5. Glue one heart-shaped fold on the other and place the remaining teardrop fold at the m-shaped part of the glued heart shapes.

6. Create an open coil fold and attach it to the bottom of the pendant. That will be the holder of the jump ring.

7. Attach the jump ring to the single-coil fold alongside your earring.

Gold Teardrop Earring:

It is effortless to make a beautiful gold earring. This guide walks you through making a paper-quilled teardrop earring seamlessly.

1. In this tutorial, I am using just two colors—light and dark gold. Pick your paper strip color according to preference. Moreover, you need 10 paper strips—5 light gold and 5 gold. Make each paper strip into a closed coil fold—more substantial and smaller coil folds.

2. Pinch one end of each coil fold to make a teardrop fold.

3. Wrap another color of the paper strip on each paper strips; repeat the process for all 5 folds.

4. Attach 2 teardrop folds in pairs to form a heart shape. You should have 5 teardrop folds—two heart shapes and one teardrop fold.

5. Glue one heart-shaped fold on the other and place the remaining teardrop fold at the m-shaped part of the glued heart shapes.

6. Create an open coil fold and attach it to the bottom of the pendant. That will be the holder of the jump ring.

7. Attach the jump ring to the single-coil fold alongside your earring.

Chapter 8: Ornaments (Easter; Halloween and Christmas)

Paper Quilled Snowflake

It costs a few minutes to make and hold snow in your palm. That sounds great, considering that you would love to play around with snow even in summer! The children and adults love to warble in snow. The elders may not be virile enough to jump around snow, which is why hand-crafted snow folds are preferable.

Interestingly, you require no much vigor or energy to build snow. Yes, you read that right, and you'll learn just how possible and easy it can be.

Paper quills bring our imaginations to reality, and one of such is the cold snow. Instead of packing and feeling the roof with cold snow, make quills snowflake a companion. This section quills pattern brings the snow close enough that you may not miss natural snow any longer.

I know you would love to learn this art, and I am willing to show you how it is done. Do you fear this design would be the most difficult of all you have seen so far? Trust me; your mind is playing games because the snowflake paper quills are as easy as any other easy-to-do paper quill.

With projects like this, you will learn to become a better quill artist rather than sit all day and be praising the quill creativity from others. It is time to get the praises too, and I trust you to do even better than what you find here.

Within a few minutes, these simple instructions will reconcile your curiosity and further make you a unique paper quill artist.

Materials Required for Paper Quilled Snowflake:

- A pair of scissors
- Quilling paper strips (blue and white)
- Pencil
- Quilling glue
- Glue dispenser
- Quilling pins
- Geometric compass
- Quilling tool
- Ruler
- A plain paper sheet

Quilled Snowflake Folds:

Here are the number of folds and types of folds needed with regards to the snowflake quilling done in this guide.

- 18 blue quarter-length tight coils
- 6 white length tight coils (54cm)
- 6 white length marquis (54cm)
- 6 blue length teardrops (54cm)
- 6 blue half-length tight coils
- 6 white quarter-length marquis
- 1 white half-length tight coils

How to Make Paper Quilled Snowflake Ornaments:

1. Paper length/width: 54cm x 5mm

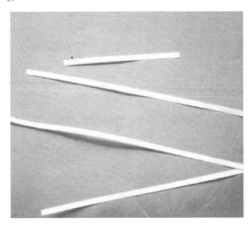

Pick a length that best suits the occasion. In this project, we are using 5mm-wide and 54cm-long paper strips. Depending on your requirement, you may opt for something different. However, for this task's purpose, use a paper strip of 5mm-wide and 54cm-long to follow up better. Use a ruler to measure the length for perfection, carefully.

2. Create a circle on the white paper

Insert the pencil and carefully stretch the compass about 5cm to 6cm-wide. Place the compass at the center of the white sheet and carefully rule a perfect circle. Finally, use the pencil to divide the circle into six visible equal parts.

3. Drawing the floral

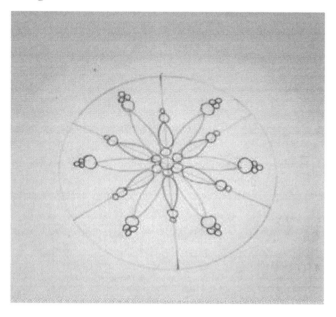

It may be difficult for a beginner to draw the floral. For now, make exactly the design you find here unless you are an expert willing to do something different. To come up with the snowflake design, you may visit online guides on how to draw a snowflake because several models could be used to develop the project. If you are okay with what is on this photo, then follow suit. You can achieve the decorative effect by doing the following:

- Draw a half-cm circle at the center of the larger circle.
- Draw 6 small circles around the small circle.

- As in the picture above, draw 6 more oval-like shapes.
- Make another 6 longer oval-like shapes round the 6 small circles.
- At the tip of the shorter oval-like shapes, create a large and a small circle as in the picture.
- Create four more circles at the tip of the 6 longer oval-like shapes, as in the picture.

4. Crafting the various folds

In this project, I am using three different paper folds including marquis, coil, and teardrop folds.

Crafting the marquis folds:

The marquis fold is an eye-shaped fold that involves pressurizing both ends of the folded quilling paper for the marquis effect.

Fold all 6 of the 54cm-long white marquis around the quilling tool or any available tool. Withdraw the quilling tool and pad each of the 6 folds gently with your fingers.

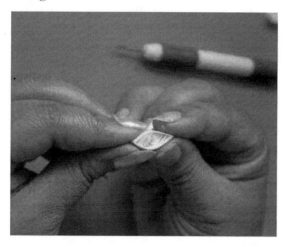

Press both ends of each white 54cm folds gently until you achieve an eye-shape. Release the pressure for the fold to loosen, pick and apply glue to the edge of the fold.

Crafting the coil folds:

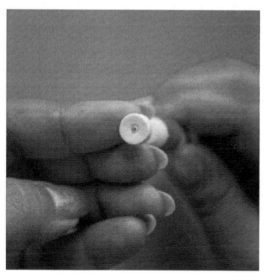

Wrap a 54cm fold around the quilling tool.

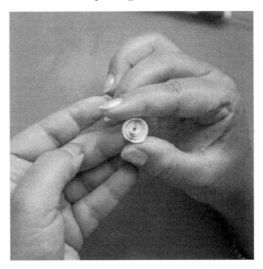

Retrieve the quilling tool and glue the flapping edge of the fold.

Crafting the teardrop folds:

Wrap a new fold around the quilling tool. Retrieve the quilling tool and release the fold to loosen.

Firmly hold one end of the fold to create a tip-like design as in the picture and apply it to the flapping edge.

5. Applying folds to the drawing

Try to place the marquis, teardrop, and coil folds in the corresponding areas of the circle. Make sure they each match the diagram, or it may distort the design.

Place each fold on the corresponding shape on the circle. Begin with the central coil fold, followed by the surrounding circular coil folds.

Place all 6 marquis folds, followed by all 6 teardrop folds in their corresponding positions. Repeat the process for the coil folds by placing a coil fold on each of the teardrop folds.

Place the remaining coil folds on the corresponding positions surrounding the teardrop and marquis folds. Place the half-done snowflake paper quill on a flat surface and apply glue to each fold carefully. Allow the glue to dry, and your lovely snowflake is ready.

You may optionally coat with a sealant to protect against water. Send your paper quills to loved ones as winter or summer gifts. During winter, make as many snowflake quills as possible and decorate your surrounding with them.

Guess what? Your crafted snowflake paper quilling can stay for as long as you desire; so far, you handle with care and coat with sealant.

Peacock Design

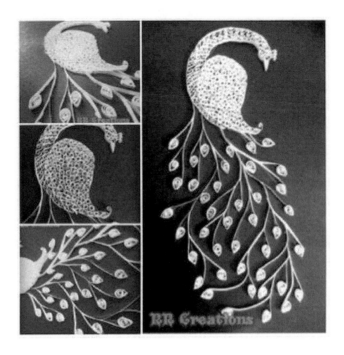

Structuring a peacock follows a similar methodology of drawing and plotting. It relies upon the quilling strip used and the mix. In the event that you need to get the specific design on the spread picture of this book, then you need to consolidate different strips to accomplish a similar outcome.

Since this is a novice's guide, we will use a single shading strip. At the point when you become sure of your aptitudes, you would then be able to continue making delightful shading mixes.

Materials Required for Peacock Design:

- Quilling strips (5mm—cream or white-hued)
- Black thick paper
- Craft paste
- Scissors
- White shading pencil
- Quilling device

When you have all these, you are prepared to begin this stunning project.

Step 1: Getting started.

Next is to draw the unpleasant blueprint of the peacock's body close by its quills. This would give you a harsh thought of what number of quilled parchments would be required and would likewise help in making staying more straightforward.

When you are finished with the necessary number you'd like, create them and checkout if it fits. Whenever happy with the result you have, feel free to stick them solidly.

Step 2: Making the neck of peacock

For the neck, I used the beehive technique of paper quilling. This may take a bit of time and requires tolerance. Cautiously organize and stick the quilled strips to each line in turn.

Step 3: Outlining

When you've finished the body and neck of the peacock, and the stick strip has dried, apply the paste and run a sort of piece along the outskirt to give a shape to the work as outlined previously.

Step 4: Connecting the Feathers

Measure the lines between each quill independently, slice and take advantage of the plume—associating every in a steady progression.

This is entirely troublesome—however, with caution and persistence, you'd accomplish it.

Step 5: It's done!!!!

You can use this as a casing to enhance your divider or as a gift to somebody exceptional.

Isn't it lovely?

Paper Quilled Christmas Wreath Ornament

The Christmas tree can't find its splendor on a Christmas without the famous green wreath. When the tree lights up, especially during a cold night, the tree beguiles the sight of every human, and the wreath stands out so uniquely.

Again, it will be splendorous to adorn the Christmas tree with the wreath.

The paper quilling art is an elite class of art on its own. Most interestingly, we can bring the green wreath to life with a couple of paper strips, glue and a quilling tool. This guide discloses the beginner basics of adequately creating a DIY wreath ornament.

It's quite an easy art to create; let's find out how.

Materials Required for Paper Quilled Christmas Wreath:

- Paper strips—light green, dark green, and red colors.
- Craft glue
- Slotted quilling tool

How to Make the Paper Quilled Christmas Wreath:

Step 1: Make dark green closed coils:

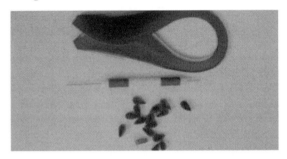

Curl the dark green strips around the slotted quilling tool to a closed coil fold. Pinch one end of the fold to make a teardrop fold (petal-like shape).

Note: About 15 teardrop folds would be enough for a mini Christmas wreath.

Step 2: Arrange the dark green teardrop folds:

Arrange the teardrop folds in a circle as in the picture above and glue the folds together to make a rounded wreath.

Step 3: Add the red and light green teardrop folds

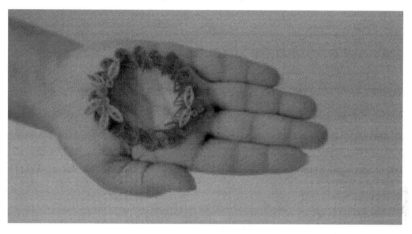

Just like the dark green teardrop fold, design the red and light green teardrop folds. Make the red folds and light green folds come in small and large sizes. Glue some read teardrop folds at the top and down part of the wreath.

You now have a great wreath! Take photos of the wreath and share it across social media platforms. You may as well use the garland to decorate your office desk, send as a card to loved ones or place it in a visible place for its charming beauty.

Christmas Time

The Christmas season is always here, and alongside it comes the yearly race to convey and part with occasion cards to your loved ones. Regarding Christmas cards, a few of us like to go with the old reserve box sets (JAM offers a few exquisite choices) while others like to take the custom-made course. If you are more inclined to place yourself into the latter classification, this post is for you.

The individuals who stay up with the latest with paper-making patterns are presumably acquainted with quilling. For the individuals who are not, here is a short clarification. Quilling is the act of twisting and molding portions of the paper to make bigger ornamental shapes and plans. Here, I will tell you the best way to use quilling to make your own delightful and brightening Christmas wreath cards!

You Will Need:

- One standard quilling instrument (A sewing needle will likewise work.)
- Bright hue red paper
- Dark red paper
- White paper or cardstock
- Scissors
- One hot glue gun (with glue)

Instructions:

Step 1:

Cut slim, 11-inch-long portions of green paper. These strips should be generally even in width. However, they shouldn't be exact.

Step 2:

Utilizing your quilling device or needle, fold the initial segment of paper into a winding. After it is completely moved, eliminate it from the device and let it mostly disentangle. It should resemble this.

Paste the remaining detail of the twisting set up with your paste firearm. Repeat this progression until you have enough green twisting's to frame a full wreath.

Step 3:

Pick a sheet of paper or card stock to use as the body of your card. For sturdiness, card stock is suggested. Before sticking it set up, lay put your green twisting's on your card surface as you might want to show up in your completed item.

After your design has been decided, use your glue gun to glue your wreath together on the card's surface!

Step 4:

Since your fundamental wreath shape is finished, you can proceed onward to making the bow. To start the bow, cut a few red and dim red paper pieces, as you did with the green paper in step 1. After these strips have been cut, pick two similar tone segments to make them into quilled tear shapes. These will turn into the inward most bits of the bow.

Step 5:

To make a teardrop shape, wind your segment of paper around the quilling instrument or needle, similar to what you did to make basic circles. While eliminating the paper from the device, just allow it to disentangle part way instead of releasing it. How much you allow it to disentangle will influence the size of your tear shape.

After this winding has completely loosened, hold the central point of this twisting with the forefinger and thumb of your non-dominant hand while pulling tenderly outward. Use your dominant hand to pull the external bit of the twisting the other way while squeezing to shape a point (the head of the tear). Paste the remaining detail of the shape set up with your glue gun.

Step 6:

After you have made two teardrop shapes of a similar tone, take two pieces of other shapes of red and firmly fold them over these shapes. Paste the remaining details set up. Next, take two portions of the main shade of red you used and freely fold them over the external surface of the shapes you just wrapped. Squeeze the head of everyone, so it coordinates the states of the focal points. To complete the two parts of the bow's head, do this again with the contrary shade of red. Shown below is the teardrop shape you began contrasted with a finished portion of a bow.

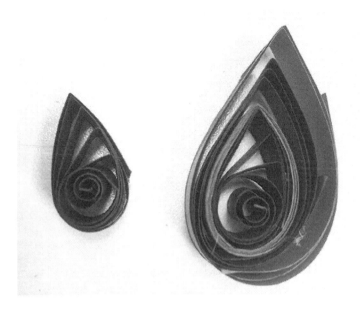

Step 7:

Make center for your bow by winding a tight, little hover of red paper and wrapping a piece of the other red shade around it. Paste this round shape along with your glue gun, and afterward, stick all lace pieces onto the wreath in any size you want!

After these are in place, loosely curl a few more red strips of paper and glue them in place to create the bottom/excess bowstrings.

Your wreath card is now complete! If you wish, you may use writing utensils to include a message such as "Merry Christmas," "Happy Holidays," or "Hi, Mom" within the wreath!

We hope that this craft helped to brighten up your season. Happy Holidays for all of us!

Christmas Tree

Supplies Needed:

- Green craft paper
- Quilling strips in different colors
- Quilling tool
- Pencil or pen
- Scissors
- Glue or glue stick

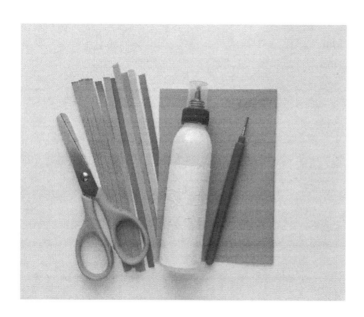

Instructions for Making the Paper Quilling Christmas Tree Ornament:

1. Take 6-inches-long green quilling strip and use the opened quilling instrument to loop the whole strip into a tight curl.

2. Separate the coiled strip from the tool and allow it to loosen up a little. Prepare a total of 15 similar loose coils.

3. Use3.5-inches red strips to make little tear shapes.

4. Now, make a couple of loops utilizing quilling strips in arranged tones. You can make them free or tight—whatever you like. Make four earthy colored free loops too.

5. Take a rectangular bit of green specialty paper and accumulate all the green free loops arranged in steps 1 and 2. Use the paste to stick 5 free curls in an orderly fashion towards the lower side of the green-hued make paper.

6. Keep staying lines of the free green curls, one over the other. As you move upward, continue lessening the number of curls in a line by 1, so you end up with a triangle design.

7. Stick the red tear shapes on the top end of the triangle. Paste them along with the pointy end out, so you get a 5-point star design.

8. Cut the art paper along the Christmas tree's external edge, including the red star.
9. Use the various brilliant loops to embellish the tree by essentially sticking them on either side. Include four earthy colored curls on the tree's base side in a square example to make the tree trunk.
10. At long last, include a little globule as the focal point of the star design if you like. Allow it to dry, and it's finished!

This quilling Christmas tree ornament is very multipurpose. You can join a string and balance it on the tree with a similarly adorable paper quilled wreath ornament. However, you can likewise make a handcrafted Christmas card with it. Or then again, why not connect it to a piece of card to cause it to go with these Christmas gift tags? It couldn't be any more obvious; a little exertion and a couple of strips sure go far!

Snowman

Christmas crafts are popular and good gifts. Right now, I will tell you how to create a Christmas paper quilling snowman.

There are many quilling paper Christmas ornaments on Panda hall. Most of them are cute and uncomplicated to make. The materials are quilling papers in different colors and some pearl beads. You need no other professional skills in making this DIY snowman craft.

Supplies Needed:

- 3mm pearl beads
- Quilling paper (bright red, green, yellow, black, white)
- Model
- Scissor
- Tweezers
- White glue
- Rolling pen

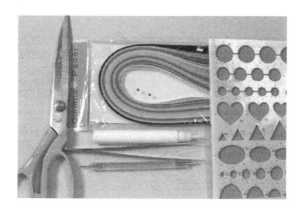

Step 1: Make a few paper quilling roundabout globules

Take around 4 pieces of white quilling papers, fold them into enormous round dabs, and stick the end solidly. Take around 2 pieces of white quilling papers, fold them into a round globule. Make the other 5 white roundabout dabs and other 2 red round dots, and 2 green roundabout dots with a similar length. Stick all the little roundabout globules around the large round dab as shown in the picture.

Step 2: Include another roundabout example and pearl dots

Roll a white roundabout dot with around 3 pieces of quilling papers; stick 2 pieces of 3mm blue pearl dabs on it as eyes. Cut an off bit of yellow quilling paper, move it to a round globule, make sure the internal part is higher than the external part.

Step 3: Make an oval bead

Fold a dark quilling paper into a roundabout globule, placed it into the 10cm opening and stick the end, and squeeze the roundabout dot into an oval dab.

Stage 4: Make the final Christmas snowman plan

Stick the dark oval dot to the top of the snowman as a cap; at that point, roll other dark round dots as shown in the picture. Cut off red quilling paper and dark quilling paper, move them a few circles and loosen them to make them look as in the image. Stick the end of the red quilling paper with the dark quilling paper together. Stick the end to the left round globules of the snowman, and stick 3 blue pearl dots on the enormous roundabout dab, as in the picture.

Here is the last look of the Christmas paper quilling snowman:

Do you love this bright and charming paper-quilling snowman? I completed this DIY snowman in 15minutes. You can likewise find it out how to make a Christmas snowman at home. It fits for another person to begin his/her quilling paper DIY project. Now, my instructional exercise on the most proficient method to make a Christmas snowman has concluded. Have a pleasant attempt!

Christmas Lights

Is it safe to say that you are searching for a novel subject to do with your children? It would even be an extraordinary subject to do with kids for a winter or Christmas celebration. With only a couple of devices, they can make this remarkable arrangement of lights to show for these special seasons!

List of Supplies:

1. Craft paper, white
2. Quilling strips
3. Slotted paper quilling tools
4. Scissors
5. Craft glue or glue stick

Instructions to make the craft:

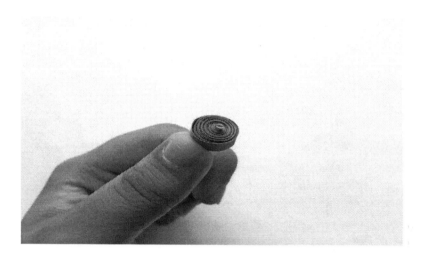

Step 1: Take 20 inches hued quilling strip, and use the opened quilling device to curl the whole strip.

Step 2: Once the coiling is finished, take out the tool's coiled strip and let it out.

Step 3: Hold any one side of the release coil to form a teardrop shape and paste the open end to secure the shape.

Step 4: Take 3-inches-long white shaded quilling strip and make a free loop shape with it.

Step 5: Press 2 inverse sides of the free curl to frame a focal point shape.

Step 6: Get the tear shape arranged in the last advances.

Step 7: Supplement the focal point shape made in step5 into the tear shape, through the hole of any loops close to the bent end; the bulb design is prepared. Also, make more bulb designs.

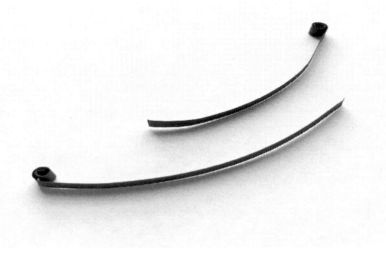

Step 8: Now, take 6-inches-long dark quilling strip and make a little whirl on any of its ends. Use around 2 or 3 cm to make the whirl design.

Step 9: Cut out a white specialty paper or cardstock paper for the foundation, or you can pick any shading you need.

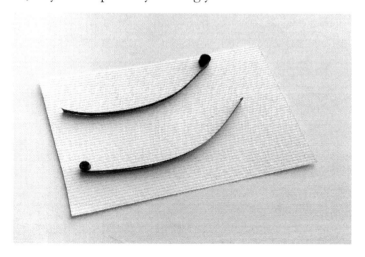

Step 10: Paste the two dark whirled strips on the paper by making a slight breathtaking example with them. Paste the two strips in 2 lines, keeping, always, 1-inch hole between them.

Step 11: Take a bulb example and paste it on the paper by keeping the bent end contiguous with the dark strip (the bulbs' fundamental wire).

Step 12: Individually include the remainder of the bulbs to fill the dark strip.

Allow the glue to dry, and have fun!

Chapter 9: Home

Paper Quilled Teardrop Vase

Your vase is beautiful, but you can enhance the beauty by making it into something alluring with paper quilling art. It is quite simple, and a matter of quilling folds into teardrops using at least four different colors if you desire a gradient effect.

This guide discloses a simplistic way of fashioning a vase with the paper-quilling art. In a matter of minutes, your first ever-alluring quilled teardrop vase should be ready.

Required Materials:

- Paper Strips

In this guide, I am using a small set of paper strips with gradient colors. You may use one color, but you won't achieve the gradient effect.

- Vase

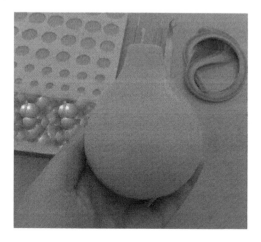

The vase must not be too curvy. It will be challenging to place the teardrop folds on an overly curvy jar. Get something smooth, and that would support the placement of folds.

- Paper glue

The glue must be such that it can glue the quilled paper on ceramic.

- Quilling needle

A cocktail stick wouldn't be a bad idea, but a quilling needle is ideal.

- Quilling board

The quilling board comes in various sizes. Depending on the size you would prefer, get a quilling board for the paper quill. Alternatively, you may use create circles on a plain sheet and use it to determine the sizes of each of the folds you make.

- Slotted quilling tool

Necessary to make folds. You can alternatively use a chewing stick.

How to Make Paper Quilled Teardrop Vase:

1. Create Coil Folds

Pick and place each quilling paper on the quilling tool. Try to make the placement at the tip of the quilling tool to be able to control the spiral shape.

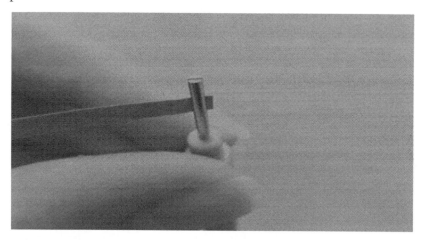

Fold each coil around the quilling tool carefully.

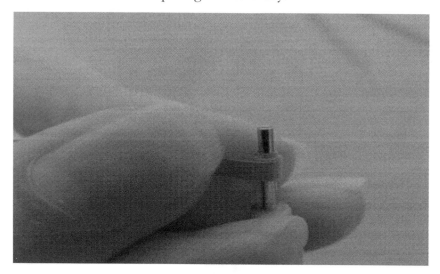

When done, hold the paper firmly but not too tight to give it excellent shape.

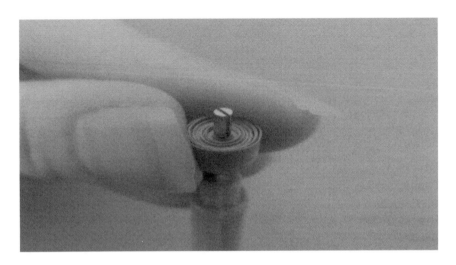

Withdraw the coil folds from the quilling tool and place them carefully in the quilling board and allow for loosening. In the absence of a quilling board, make sure that each fold fits the size of the circle you created on a plain sheet.

Repeat this process for all the quilling papers

2. Make the teardrop effect

Withdraw each of the coil folds from the quilling board.

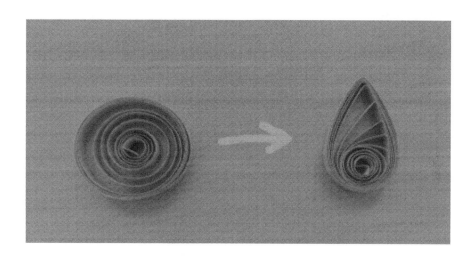

Place your two fingers at one end of the coil fold.

Gently, press that end to form a tip.

Hold it tight with added pressure.

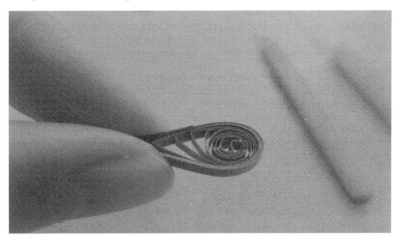

You should now have a well-made teardrop fold.

Place the teardrop fold on the quilling board and repeat the process for every paper.

3. Decorate the Vase with the Teardrop Folds

Pick up, clean your vase, and arrange the teardrop folds according to their colors.

Beginning from the bottom of the vase, apply paper glue to the teardrop folds and glue each fold to the jar.

Continue the gluing process and fill up the bottom of the vase. A darker fold color is preferable if you're beginning from the bottom of the vessel.

Repeat the gluing process for the second row of the vase. This time, the color of the fold should be lighter than the color of the fold at the bottom for the gradient effect.

Again, attach each teardrop fold to the vase in the third row. Try to use a color different from that of the second row, as in the picture above.

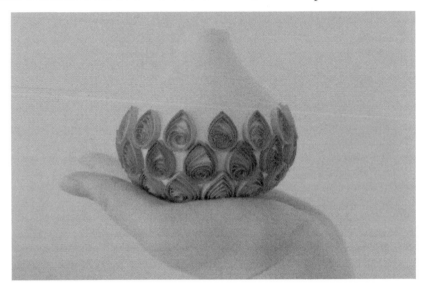

Finally, use a lighter color for the fourth row to complete the gradient effect.

You now have a lovely quilled teardrop vase.

Note: Depending on the size of your vase, you may attach teardrop folds for more than four rows. If you intend to cover the entire vessel with the teardrop drops, endeavor to resize the teardrop folds when you reach the curvy part of the vessel. Retaining the longer teardrops will result in a distorted quilling in that area.

Now that you have an elegantly-crafted quilled teardrop vase, you may send it across to loved ones or share your knowledge with friends.

Paper Quilled Flower Frame

Materials Required:

- Quilling tool (any of your choice)
- Paper quilling strip (we'll be using different colors, feel free to use any color of your choice, here I used blue, purple, white, yellow)
- Glue
- Paper swab or toothpick (for applying the glue)
- Pearls

Directions:

1. Make as many teardrops as you can, some bigger than some (three different sizes of teardrops, the bigger ones should be more with different colors).

2. Equally, make lots of marquis shape and closed coils.

3. Now attached the pointed ends of the bigger teardrops in groups of six using the glue, do the same for the other marquis, matching the same colors together. Make enough flowers to go around your frame completely.

4. Now attach the pearl to the mid-point of each created flower.

5. Place this around your frame and glue it in place.

6. Next, fill up the spaces between using the marquis and glue them in place.

7. Next, use the closed coil to fill up the even smaller spaces left and also glue it in place. Voila, your frame is ready. You can place a greeting card in the middle, or even place the picture of a loved one there.

3D Flowers

It's time to step up your game a little as beginners as we'll be designing a 3-D flower from scratch.

Materials Required:

    a. Paper strips (different colors)

    b. Quilling tool

    c. Tweezers

    d. Glue

Directions:

1. Create lots of marquis and further convert most of it into a slug.

2. Now attach these in groups of three (same colors), place the elongated marquis at the middle and the slugs at the sides, use the glue and hold until its dried, repeat these for all the

created marquis and slugs, now wrap each group of 3 with a different color of the paper strip.

3. You should have 17 petals in total.

4. Arrange them in groups of 5 attaching the pointed ends with the glue.

5. Now make 3 large closed coils with variations of colored paper strips as illustrated, make it as large as you like.

6. Apply glue to one side of each closed coils and place it in the middle of the arranged group of 5 flower petals.

7. To have the desired 3-D effect, place the flower on your palm and press the middle with the attached closed coil inward.

8. Using glue, attach different shades of paper strips to form a stronger bond of the paper strip, use as many colored strips as you want.

9. When it is thick enough, use a tweezer to coil the ends of the modified paper strip. This forms the tendrils.

10. Make two shorter versions of this without coiling.

11. Place two uncoiled short tendrils at 90° to each other, facing upward. Then place the coiled tendril in the middle.

12. Next, use the glue to attach 3 slugs to one of the uncoiled tendrils, place the 2 green petals at the top of the other uncoiled tendril and finally place the last slug at the point where the curve starts beside the coiled tendril.

13. Now place your prepared flowers at the bottom of the tendrils arranging them as illustrated. And that's it, your 3-D flower is ready.

Chapter 10: Gifts

Quilled Butterfly Pendant

1. Make paper strips of different colors into teardrop folds. As in the picture above, make the folds into big and smaller sizes.

2. Arrange the teardrop folds into a butterfly shape as in the picture above, glue them together and allow them to dry.

3. Coat the quilled pendant and allow it to dry.

4. Finally, fit in the jumping ring, and attach to a necklace.

Paper Quilling Dolls

Materials:

- Color papers (paper weights 130-180grams)
- 3mm (1/8") and 6.5mm (1/4") color paper strips (paper weights 130-180grams)
- Different lengths and thicknesses of the strip may require more or less strips to make the same circle size. I used the 21.5 x 27.9cm (8.5 x 11") cardstock papers which weigh 176grams to cut pieces.
- This type of paper strip maybe tricky to find. You can use a knife or trimmer to cut the paper into strips. I think the most convenient and fastest way is to use shredders (size 6.5mm (1/4") and 3mm (1/8") strip-cut).
- Poster paper (use for making the base, or you can use other paper instead).

Tools:

- Slotted quilling tool
- White glue
- Scissors
- Ruler
- Utility knife
- Cutting mat

Optional tools:

- Circle sizer ruler
- Mini mold
- Size 6.5mm (1/4") and 3mm

- (1/8") strip-cut shredder
- Paper trimmer
- Bow punch and hole punch
- Tweezers
- Paintbrush
- Bamboo sticks

1.1 Making the Base:

(A tight circle)

Prepare a white poster paper 55.8cm x 71.1cm (22" x 28"). Cut the white poster paper into 6.5mm x 55.8cm strips.

A paper shredder provides a convenient and fast way to make quilling strips. If you don't have a shredder, you can use a utility knife or other cutting tools to cut.

171

Using a thicker and longer poster paper can save time when rolling the circles.

1. Apply a tiny amount of glue at the end of the strips.
    If you accidentally put too much on, you can use a toothpick or brush to apply evenly.

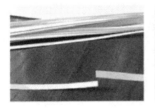

2. Glue 9 strips end to end to make a long strip.

3. Turn it in a way that makes you feel comfortable. You can place your thumb and index finger on both sides of the paper strip to keep it neat.

4. Maintain tension on the paper strip while you are rolling. When the piece is fully gone, gently pull the tool off. Don't let it expand. Pull it tight.

5. Apply a small amount of glue on the end. Hold it for a few seconds until the glue is dried. Now, we have a tight circle with a diameter of 4.2cm.

6. Squeeze the glue on the circle, and use a brush to apply it evenly. Wait for it to dry, then the base is done.

1.2 Making Basic Head Shape:

To make a head, you need 3mm (1/8") wide skin-colored strips. You can use a mini shredder or another cutting tool to cut skin-colored paper.

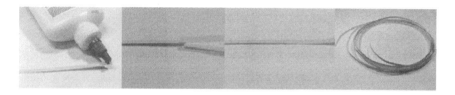

1. Glue 13 strips end to end to make a long strip (Different lengths and thicknesses of the strip will need different numbers of pieces to make the same circle size). Make two long strips.

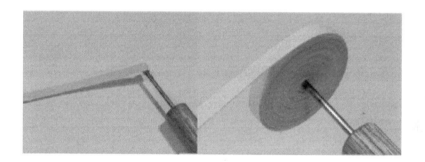

2. Use the tool to roll the long strip to make a tight circle with a diameter of 3.2cm.

After, pulling the circle tight, glue the end and hold it for a few seconds until the glue dries.

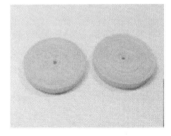

One head requires 2 tight circles.

3. Use your fingers or mini mold to push gently on the tight circle, shaping it into a dome as shown. Make 2 of them.

4. To make sure the domes do not collapse, coat them with a layer of glue on the inside. Let it dry.

5. Apply glue around the edge of each dome. Place the 2 dome edges together and press closed. Make sure it is even all the way around. Let it dry.

6. Apply glue all the way around the joint, then take a strip of paper and glue it all around. When you have gone around once cut the remaining piece and glue the end. Your basic head shape is now finished.

1.3 Making a Student Doll:

Materials:

- 3mm (1/8") wide skin-colored paper strips (28)
- 3mm (1/8") wide blue-colored paper strips (5)
- 6.5mm (1/4") wide light blue-colored paper strips (10)
- 6.5mm (1/4") wide blue-colored paper strips (7)
- 6.5mm (1/4") wide brown-colored paper strips (3)
- 6.5mm (1/4") wide green-colored paper strips (8)
- 2.5cm wide green-colored paper strips (2)
- 2.5cm wide creamy-colored paper strip (1)
- 2.8cm wide orange-colored paper strip (1/2)
- 1 base
- 2 small eyes (use the 2mm hole punch or use scissors.)

Making the Student's Doll Head:

1. Make a basic head shape using the 28 pieces of 3mm (1/8") wide skin-colored paper strips (Please see and follow the instruction in 1.2 Making Basic Head Shape).

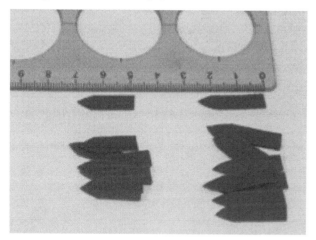

2. Cut the three 6.5mm wide brown colored strips into 2.5cm-long and 2cm-long pieces.

3. Use the hole left from the quilling tool to be a nose. Stick a 2.5cm-long strip on the lower part of the head and then stick another one overlapping the first one slightly. Repeat all the steps till you finish the semicircle.

4. Stick the 2cm-long strips on the face to become bangs. Leave the points free of glue.

5. Use the remaining strips to stick on the upper part of the head as shown. Leave the points without glue.

6. Stick the strips on top of the head as shown, leaving the points without glue. Use the fingers to fold up the ends to make them feel like upturned hair.

Making the Student's Doll Body:

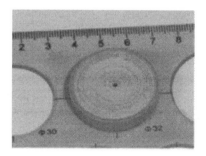 

1. Glue ten 6.5mm-wide strips of light blue and three 6.5mm-wide pieces of blue end to end to make a long strip. Use the long piece to make a tight circle with a diameter of 3.2cm.
   Note: When making a circle or cylinder, always glue the end.
2. Use fingers gently pushing up the quilled paper into the ruler as shown in the picture.

 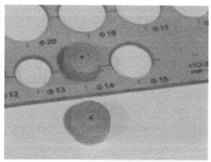

3. Use two 6.5mm-wide strips of a circle and create a cone shape around blue to make a tight circle with a height of 4 cm. Concave the point with a diameter of 1.4cm. Make 2 of the cones slightly to help stick them to the head.

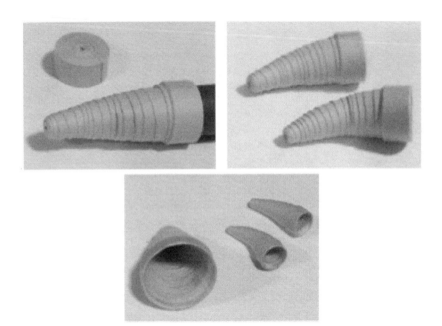

4. Use a pen gently pushing out the circles and create cone shapes around 3.5cm-tall as shown. Then slightly Coat the inside of the bend the sleeves. Body and envelopes with glue. Let dry.

Assembling the Body and Making a Student's Book:

1. Glue the head, body and sleeves together. Let dry.

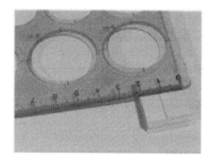 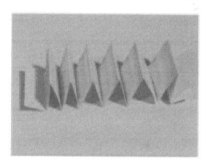

2. Fold the 2.5cm-wide milky-colored strip back and forth in 2cm increments as shown. This will be the pages.

3. Fold the 2.8cm-wide orange-colored strip around the pages as shown. Make sure the two ends come together evenly. Cut off the excess.

4. Glue the pages and cover together as shown.

Making the Hood:

1. Glue four 3mm-wide strips of blue end to end to make gently flatten the cone.

2. Use this strip to make a tight circle with a diameter of 2cm gently push up the ring and create a collapse. Coat the cone shape, as shown, inside with glue.

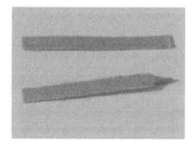

3. Use a 3mm-wide blue-colored strip to cut two 3cm-long pieces. Pinch one end, and glue the other end into the hood.

4. Glue the book at the front of the body and the hood at the back as shown. Let dry.

Making the Student Doll's Legs:

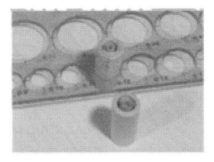

1. Roll the two 2.5cm-wide green-colored strips into two cylinders with a diameter of 1.2cm as shown.

2. Apply a tiny amount of glue at the end of a 6.5mm-wide green-colored strip. Attach it to the end of the cylinder and wrap it around making an outer ring. Pull up the circle as shown and coat the inside with glue.

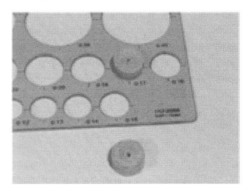

3. Glue three 6.5mm-wide green-colored strips together and make it into a tight circle with a diameter of 1.7cm. Make 2.

4. Glue the cylinders on the circles. Let dry. Now two legs are complete.

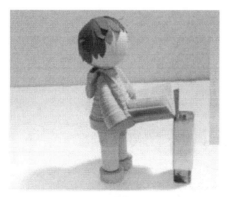

5. Glue the legs to the body (Support until dry).

Making the Student Doll's Hands:

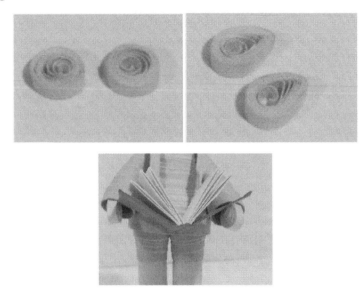

1. Roll a 3mm-wide skin-colored strip into a loose circle with a diameter of 1.2cm and glue the end. Pinch one side of the ring to make a teardrop. Make 2 of them. Glue them into the sleeves as hands.

2. Finally, glue the eyes to the face and stick the doll on the base. Now your student quilling doll is completed.

188

Chapter 11: Other Paper Quilling Projects

Paper Crafts-Quilled Butterfly Headband

Materials Required:

- Shaded cardstock (one sheet every one of dim purple, light purple, white, and pink)
- Toothpicks
- Paste
- Mod
- Quilling device
- Scissors
- Gemstones in pink and purple

- Sparkle
- Plastic paste
- Headband

I printed out a thought of my motivation a delightful pink and purple butterfly. Also, gathered together my devices. For this undertaking, I used a little quilling device. You can discover them at most art stores. I trust I paid only a couple of dollars for this device and I've used it for a considerable period of time! Likewise, I like to use Aleene's Tacky Glue on the grounds that merely like it says in the name, it is cheap. I can work considerably more rapidly as the paste works quickly and dries clear.

I can work considerably more rapidly as the paste works quickly and dries clear.

I used my little paper shaper to cut around 5 every (1/8") segment of each shading. On the off chance that you don't possess a paper shaper, you can surely do this with scissors.

Start by sliding the finish of a pink strip into the space of the quilling device. At that point, bend the instrument and start winding the paper strip around the end of the device.

Curve the device and wind the paper until the whole strip is twisted around the end of the instrument. Handle the edges of the paper and slide the device out. You currently have a decent winding.

Squeeze one finish of the winding to make a tear shape and include a spot of crude paste to the furthest limit of the paper strip. You now have one tear drop formed winding.

Make one more tear formed winding in pink, and afterward 2 spirals that are squeezed at each end. Paste each pair together as appeared. Take some of the light purples and include dabs of paste along its length. Use that light purple strip to fold over a lot of pink spirals. Repeat with the next set.

Utilize a similar strategy to make four dull purple spirals. Paste them together. Enclose the upper pink wings with dim purple strips like you did the light purple.

Include light purple strips around the dim purple wings, and afterward include white pieces around every one of the four sides. Now, slice a toothpick to the length that you might want the body to be.

Stick along some of the dim purples and wind it around the toothpick, absolutely covering it. Paste the wings to one another and to the sides of the toothpick as appeared. Cut two 1/16" extensive portions of dim purple for the receiving wires, and loop the end with your quilling device. Paste-on.

Spot the butterfly on plastic (so it won't stick) and coat it with Mod Podge for security. When dry, flip it over and cover the opposite side. Allow it to dry completely. Include a couple of stick gems for shimmer. At that point, include specks of paste along the edges of the wings and sprinkle sparkle to finish the look. Tap off the additional sparkle and allow to dry

And there you have it. A lovely shimmering butterflies! You can do loads of things with this little paper animal. You can enhance a casing with it, cause a cooler magnet, to make divider craftsmanship, or do as I do and make a headband out of it.

Quilled Flower Locket

Materials Required:

- Quilling paper—dark, (1/8-inch standard width strips) or slice your own light to medium weight paper utilizing an art blade, metal-edged ruler, and cutting mat
- Quilling instrument—opened device or needle device or substitute a hardened wire or even a biscuit analyzer
- Scissors
- Ruler
- Tweezers
- Paper penetrating device or mixed drink stick—to apply stick
- T-pin or glass head pin—to shape blossom focus
- Non-stick surface—use as paste palette and work board. An acrylic sheet, waxed paper, or Styrofoam plate are fine as well; I for the most part use a container top
- Clammy material—clingy stick fingers and quilling don't blend
- Gems pincers—2, mine are level nose

192

- Bounce ring—silver
- Memento—silver (the one I used is from Michaels; read progressively about it in Part 1)
- Strip—3/8-inch width; around 24 inches

Directions:

1. Make the blossom: roll a 3-inch dark tight loop on quilling instrument of decision. (You'll discover more data about picking a device in Part 1) Glue end set up before slipping curl off the device. Tip: if the strip has a torn period, the paper will follow easily when stuck, making the loop look overall quite round.

   Shape the loop top by squeezing a T-pin or a glass head pin against one side to make an adjusted vault.

   At that point apply a modest quantity of paste inside the arch to save the bend.

2. Make 10 matching ring windings by wrapping a length of quilling paper multiple times around a dowel. Test with various dowels to figure out which one creates the right curl size for the pendant you are using. Most likely one of your device handles will work; I used a paper piercer.

   Slide loop off the dowel, fix it if necessary by pulling the strip end, and squeezing one spot to make a tear shape. You'll feel embarrassingly clumsy from the start with the wrapping/sliding/squeezing, yet after a little practice, it turns out to be natural.

   Paste end and trim overabundance paper.

3. On a non-stick work board, stick tips of tear petals around the domed focus taking consideration to space them equally.

4. Whenever the paste has gotten an opportunity to set for a few minutes, apply a slender covering of glue to the rear of the bloom with a fingertip or mixed drink stick. Use tweezers to fixate the flower on the memento. It's ideal not to squirm it into position as this will leave a snail trail of paste. Allow the blossom to dry for the time being... make an effort not to be impatient.

5. The following day, turn open a bounce ring with forceps and slip it through the fixed memento ring.
Close hop ring and string onto the strip. Polish off with a customizable sliding bunch so the neckband can be slipped here and there over the head.

The memento is prepared to wear or provide for somebody on your vacation list; maybe a little youngster who may be roused to have a go at quilling as well. Children for the most part love to plume!

Chapter 12: How to Preserve Your Paper Quilling Projects

I know what it takes to complete a single project and no new or advanced crafter can afford to let the plan get ruined. However, this preservative method is split into two sections so we can attend to 2D and 3D designs separately. But in the end, you should be able to choose the technique you feel you are okay with.

Preservative Methods for 2D Quilled Projects

Plastic Sheet

This is one of the most natural techniques to preserve your quilled paper project. It has an opening made with OHP transparent sheet and frame that accommodates your craft.

With this, you are sure your coils are fully protected from dust and getting pressed with a heavy landing. Simply check any stationary shop around your neighborhood to get these OHP sheets.

Varnish Spray

Though this might be a little bit expensive compared to the first method, it keeps your projects clean and polished. It enables the quilling paper to become stiff and dries fast but be mindful of the one you get because a bad one will alter the color of your designs. Ensure you spray at a distance of at least 15cm.You can get this in any of your craft and hobbies store near you.

Preservative Methods for 3D Quilled Projects

White Glue Coating

Fevicol is a good sample of white glue to look at because it's readily available in most stationery stores and you can easily apply this directly with a brush.

Though you can also use it for 2D projects, ensure it is smooth evenly when applying. To make it smooth, mix with a 2:1 portion of Favicol and water to make the smooth application consistent.

If the water is too much, the coil will loosen and make your project look awkward. While, if the mixture is also ticked, you are likely to damage it.

This method will make your 3D project looks elegant and improves the color of the strips. Carryout the coating more than once in 15-20 minutes to strengthen the project. Note, this sealant will act as dustproof but not water repellent. You can also find some other brands that are water-resistant and lighter in a texture that suits both 2D and 3D.

Nail Polish

This method is quite cheap and readily available at cosmetic stores. Nail polish provides an intense sheen and at the same time hardens the strips.

This is best for 3D and closed coils but don't use this for projects that are likely to be exposed to heat, sun, or water because it can melt, peel off, or even develop cracks.

Nail polish is water-resistant but not waterproof.

Now you can go on with your favorite design and pattern with the hope of using any of the above methods to keep your project alive.

Chapter 13: Striking Paper Quilling Artists

Striking and legitimate people are available in each field of life and the specialty of paper crafting itself. To give you more inspiration when making paper quilling projects, recorded underneath are the famous and legitimate world-class paper quillers, their profiles, remarks and aides for apprentices in the authority of paper quilling.

Yulia Brodskaya

The Russian craftsman is well known for her tastefulness and itemized work of art. Albeit, by and by situated in the UK, she says "typography is my second love after paper and I'm extremely upbeat that I've discovered a method of joining the two. Having said that, I would prefer not to prohibit non-grammatical mistake-based structures, I'd prefer to deal with various activities."

The research paper realistic is known to be what Yulia depicts her works, as accuracy and outright enumerating are fairly unmistakable components of them. Yulia began as an artist and visual craftsman, however changed to paper artistry after her first paper project. She expected to structure a unique presentation for her name on a handout and used paper quilling. The rest is history.

Farah Al Fardh

Farah, the Emirati craftsman is alluded to as a pioneer in the Arabic world as respects to paperwork. She is obviously the first Emirati craftsman to be respected with the privileged "Endorsement of

Accreditation" from The Paper Quilling Guild in the UK, as she visits to stun the world with her astonishing works, her fantastic enthusiasm for unusual 3D paper quilling models. I am very sure you will pay a visit to her helpful and fascinating YouTube channel.

Ashley Chiang

Yulia Brodskaya could be supposed to be the motivation to have birthed this paper quilling sensation. As indicated by Ashley here and there in December 2012, she went over Yulia's work and was shocked by the art and quickly picked incredible enthusiasm for quilling practice. Within a year, she was displaying at the stand-out show in Chicago, and from that point forward her development in paper quilling has been upward and onward as it were. Her works are interesting for sharp and splendid hues just as eye-catching structures which make her work fulfilling to take a look at. The American resident has demonstrated to be an extraordinary sensation in this field.

Ann Martin

Ann Martin is a creator and paper craftsmanship fan that works in "custom quilled marriage authentications, ketubot, and wedding greeting mats that are reasonable for confining, just as paper gems." She has a site that centers around paper quilling and different kinds of paper expressions. I especially like the site in light of the fact that Ann includes top-notch paper expressions and artisans, and is a phenomenal wellspring of data if you need to stay aware of current patterns in the realm of paper creating.

Sena Runa

The Turkish craftsman is known to be a wayfarer of new domains in artistry, as she makes for herself her particular style, which in her words gives her an opportunity. Different to most artists, she makes her own strips accordingly to her signature of all her pieces of work. She's additionally nitty-gritty with hues as she manages home designs of all sort. Every single one of Sena's structures happens to be merry as she unmistakably fuses the ink into her paper delineations. She is recorded to have sold around 180 works throughout the whole world. She owns a site which I suggest you visit and will discover fascinating and charming works.

Jitesh Patel

The Europe-based craftsman is perceived for his production of ongoing prospects that guides paper-quilling customers to get by in their unquenchable universe of structures. He is gifted and skilled in heading and delineation and unlike some other craftsmen, has thought that it was helpful to all to manufacture a library containing components for unique plans. His structures are supposed to be comprised of lines in their most straightforward structure, anyway, they are so fragile.

Bavani Ratnam

In her words "quilosophy is tied in with sharing the specialty of paper quilling" the paper quilling master who has practically been in the field since the mid-21st century is known for the production of enriching expression cards and many others. The Malaysian magnificence is said to have higher interests and dreams albeit still in the quilosophical field, she works a ton with paper, however, she's unmistakably not restricted to it.

Dr. Jiji

The Indian dental specialist holds a record for her work which entered the general records for her 101 works of paper quilling which was displayed at a presentation in Thrissur in some occasions in the first half of 2016. She started her plume project in 2012 and self-prepared in every last bit of her leisure activities, including painting, but paper quilling remains her preferred activity.

Ideally, through these little extracts of such incredible works, you'll find the motivation to plunge into the profundities of this hypnotizing paper work, and find your own exceptional paper quilling styles come to you. As intriguing as these specialists seem to be, we are sure the universe of paper quilling has a lot more.

Conclusion

Paper Quilling is extraordinarily simple. It is easy to complete. You don't need to put in a lot of your time and effort to get familiar with the exchange by any means. You should simply acquaint the fundamental aptitudes and procedures of the trade and there you have it! With a little practice and repetition, you will before long become a specialist.

The different devices and materials that are essential for this exchange are commonly less expensive to drop by. They are likewise locally accessible. You don't need to invest a lot of your energy and effort to source them from a remote place off.

On the off chance that you are continually stressed out, this craftsmanship is an extraordinary way of getting away from the distressing circumstances. Throughout working the paper strips, you get the opportunity to scatter pressure and the development of anguish. This prompts a loose and made height.

Finally, the exchange additionally adds to the incitement of the mind. This is because of the way that it improves the progression of blood in the body. Thusly, you get the opportunity to remain fresh, alert and fit as a fiddle. You may wish to give it a shot while concentrating to support your concentration and consideration.

You may well have noticed that the specialty of quilling is an incredible endeavor without a doubt. The various potential advantages it brings along are beyond any reasonable amount to disregard or treat with less reality.

This is the reason you are, by all methods, encouraged to consider checking it out on the off chance that you have never. All the best as you begin in the field of paper quilling!

One of the most significant characteristics about paper quilling is that it is fun and simple to make. When you've aced it, structuring any sorts of quilling works will be your preferred leisure activity.

There are different fascinating artworks that you can make out of quilling paper, it just takes, knowing the fundamentals, strategies, and ideas to frame designs of your choice.

The most ideal approach to begin, in the event that you are a beginner, is to discover motivation, you need to contemplate quilled craftsmanship that you want, and use it as a springboard for making your own breathtaking structures, maybe, soon enough you will be astounded how individuals will appreciate your work and use it as a motivation for their quilling projects.

Individuals who make a wide range of art using quilling paper began as a fledgling, testing and playing with various types of shapes and procedures to make simple, but viable specialty designs. When you have your blueprint, the inventive opportunity is all yours.

It's just about paper crafting that includes slender segments of paper into one-of-a-kind 3D shapes. These little paper structures can be used to finish various types of things you may be shocked about. Actually, you can make quilling designs that are complementary.

I explicitly composed this book to help you with creating abilities and methods that will cause you to make your own show-halting structures when you have learned paper quilling, which is the craft of folding and molding pieces of paper into improving plans. I can guarantee you that you will start to deliver beautiful quilled works while building your aptitudes.

This book is supplied with supportive tips and it also has adequate fundamental information to paper quilling that will empower you to practice this art without stress. It additionally gives tips for the best devices and sorts of paper to use for your quilling projects. Particularly, as a novice and the basic shape to begin with the goal for you to ace paper quilling and turn into a pro in under seven days.

It won't just instruct all of you to think about paper quilling, it will likewise hand over to you a mainstream expertise that can make a salary for you when you make your most-loved pastime and become imaginative with the artwork.

It would be ideal if you read and give me a survey of how you feel about the book. You may wish to focus on supporting your attention and thought.

Glossary

3-Dimensional Figures—an influential character or an article or shape that has three measurements—length, width and tallness

Anniversary Card—a card given to recall the date on which an occasion occurred in an earlier year.

Butterfly—a nectar-taking of creepy-crawly with two sets of enormous, normally splendidly shaded wings that are secured with minuscule scopes. Butterflies are recognized from moths by having clubbed or expanded receiving wires, holding their arms erect when very still, and being dynamic by day.

Christmas Wreath—a: a brightening course of action of foliage or blossoms on a roundabout base a Christmas wreath. b: a band of interweaved flowers or leaves worn as a characteristic of respect or triumph: festoon a tree wreath.

Coil—Loops a length of something wound or organized in a winding or arrangement of rings.

Crimper—otherwise called wire crimper, creasing instrument or pleating forceps, is a device used for creasing connectors onto wires.

Diamond—a precious stone, one side of which is level, and the other cut into twenty-four triangular sides in two territories which structure an arched face pointed at the top

Double Flower—depicts assortments of blossoms with additional petals, frequently containing blooms inside blossoms.

Gold-Plated—secured or featured with gold or something of brilliant shading. Having a satisfying or flashy appearance that hides something of minimal worth.

Happy Birthday Card—it's a welcome card given or sent to an individual to commend their birthday.

Learner—a newcomer or amateur, particularly an individual not used to the difficulties of pioneer life.

Locket—a little decorative case, regularly made of gold or silver, worn around an individual's neck on a chain and used to hold things of nostalgic worth, for example, a photo or lock of hair.

Marquis— (in some European nations) an aristocrat positioning over a tally and under a duke.

Necklace—a fancy chain or series of dots, gems, or connections worn around the neck.

Open Markets—an unhindered market with free access by and rivalry of purchasers and vendors.

Opened Circle Sizer—it's a disentangled adaptation of our circle format board with gap estimates that arranges with the entirety of our quilling packs.

Paper—material produced in dainty sheets from the mash of wood or different stringy substances, used for composing, drawing, or imprinting on, or as wrapping material.

Paper Quilling—is a work of art that includes the utilization of portions of paper that are rolled, molded, and stuck together to make enlivening plans.

Pastime—an action done consistently in one's relaxation time for joy.

Peacock—a male peafowl, which has long tail quills that have eye-like markings and can be raised and fanned out in the show.

Pre-Cut Strips—cut into size or shape before being showcased, gathered, or used: precut filet of fish; precut development materials.

Preserve—look after (something) in its unique or existing state.

Quilling Brush—looks precisely like an afro brush with metal prongs. It is used for making paper curls and paper blossoms that are prevalently used in paper quilling artistry structures and scrapbook plans.

Quilling Needle—it's one of the most generally used quilling devices. It permits you to make little focuses on rolls and parchments which creates increasingly appealing quilling.

Rolling—moving by turning again and again on a hub.

Semi-Circle—some of a hover or of its circuit.

Shredder—a machine or other gadget for destroying something, particularly archives.

Slug—an extremely cleaned earthly mollusk that ordinarily does not have a shell and secretes a film of bodily fluid for security. It very well may be a genuine plant bug.

Snowflakes—a chip of day off, a padded ice precious stone, commonly showing fragile six-fold balance.

Square Shape—a plane figure with four straight sides and four right points, particularly one with inconsistent nearby sides, as opposed to a square.

Strips—a plane figure with four equivalent straight sides and four right points.

Structure—an arrangement or attracting delivered to show the look and capacity or activities of a structure, article of clothing, or another item before it is manufactured or made.

Tear—molded like a solitary tear.

Tear—pull or tear (something) separated or to pieces with power.

Triangle—a plane figure with three straight sides and three points.

Trick—keep from developing or growing appropriately

Tulip—a bulbous spring-blooming plant of the lily family, with strikingly shaded cup-formed blossoms.

Tweezers—a little instrument that is made of two thin bits of metal which are joined toward one side and that is used to hold, move, or pull exceptionally little articles.

Valentine's Day Card—a card communicating adoration or love, sent, frequently secretly, to your darling or satirically to a companion, on Saint Valentine's Day.

Youngsters—pincers, pliers, forceps, or a comparative device for holding or cutting.

Finally, if you've found this book helpful in any way, an Amazon review is always welcome!